302

QUESTIONS & ANSWERS

For Every Savvy
Real Estate Investor

the savvy LANDLORD

Steven VanCauwenbergh
Walter Jenkins

the savvy LANDLORD

302 Questions & Answers
For Every Real Estate Investor

International Standard Book Number: 978-1-943186-00-6

Printed in the United States of America

Library of Congress Cataloging-in-Publication Data
is available from the publisher

Published by Teflon Publishing
8 NE 48th Street, Oklahoma City, OK 73105

This book is dedicated to the friends who stood by me when I went down paths that were unfamiliar and daunting. I recognize John Day for being the support legs of my table; Devin Long for being the tabletop and serving others; Kayle Grieman for her gift of reading; Shawn McVicker for his inspiration, commitment to success, and doing the right thing; Greg Meech for making sure it fits and it's the best decision; Jessica Watson for just doing it; Ed O'Toole for support and perspective; Thomas Morgan for relentless pursuit and pushing forward; Jeffery Taylor for confidence and opportunity; Liz Poteet for the grit in the sandpaper and growing smoothly; and Walter B. Jenkins for being the finisher.

CONTENTS

"Real Estate investing, even on a very small scale, remains a tried and true means of building an individual's cash flow and wealth."

– Robert Kiyosaki

INTRODUCTION

Welcome to the fourth Savvy Landlord book. If you are new to real estate investing or are considering making it your occupation, I hope this book answers some of the questions you may be asking. If you are a seasoned investor, I hope these questions will make you think about how you are building your business. At the least, I want to you be comforted by the fact that other investors face the same challenges and struggles that you do. You are not alone, and I hope you can laugh at what other investors have endured.

As always, may your next deal be your best deal.

QUESTIONS AND ANSWERS

1. I can't reconcile my checkbook. Should I be a real estate investor?

Real estate investing has given me a lifestyle I never dreamed of, and it is a great way to build a future for you and your family. I am so passionate about what it can do for people that I created the Savvy Landlord brand and have spent years telling people about why they should become investors.

To be a successful investor and build an empire that lasts decades, you need to have some ability to understand numbers. When you look at a property, you need to be able to look at the asking price, determine how much work needs to be done on the property and how much that will cost, and you need to understand what a fair rental amount for the property is.

A lot of people aren't great with numbers. I know a writer who can't balance his checkbook without Quicken. But the good news is that most of this can be done on a laptop or a smartphone. You don't have to be some freaky math genius to make money as an investor. You do need to understand what your strengths and weaknesses are, and if you aren't great at adding, dividing, and subtracting be sure to carry a calculator with you, or use the calculator app on your cell phone. Use that to crunch the numbers before you buy or pass on a property.

If you are really bad with numbers you should consider hiring a bookkeeper (which is what I do) or find online resources. Many investors use mint.com and seem happy.

2. When should I hire an accountant? What do I look for?

You should hire an accountant and an attorney before you buy your first property. Period. No exceptions. If you don't, you may leave thousands of dollars on the table in missed deductions and not have the legal protection you need because you didn't establish the best business structure for you.

Look for professionals who have experience with real estate investors. It's easy to think that because someone has passed the CPA exam or the bar exam that they are capable of handling any tax or legal issue, but one of the keys to success is working with people who specialize. A good place to find one would be at your local REIA (real estate investor association) club. In many cities, accountants and attorneys belong to specialist associations. Search the Internet to see if there are any groups near you. You might also consider searching for them on meetup.com.

3. Getting a loan from a bank seems intimidating. Is there a better way?

No investor likes dealing with banks. I am fortunate because I have built a relationship with a local bank. Because of our track record of working together, it's easier for me to have a loan approved than it is for most people, especially newbies. I know what my banker wants and how he wants it.

When you are new to investing and don't have a track record of working with a bank, or if you don't like the headache of dealing with traditional banks, there are other ways to get your deals done. One method of unconventional financing is to deal with private investors. People are realizing loaning money to real estate investors can offer higher returns than Wall Street.

Savvy investors can find private investors who are willing to loan them money to buy properties. The paperwork is not nearly as involved as using a traditional bank, but you may pay a higher return in exchange for the easy access. A great way to find unconventional financing is through a mortgage broker. You should always seek commercial money.

4. **What is a mortgagee sale?**

A mortgagee sale, also known as a foreclosure, is where a property is sold by the lender who holds the lien, which usually happens when the borrower has gone into default. The lender is trying to recoup its investment in the property.

Some people think buying property in a mortgagee sale is wrong. They don't like the idea of buying a property that is only available because someone else fell on hard times. The only thing they see is the previous owner being forced out of the property and living on the street. Don't be that investor. You didn't cause the problem, and you shouldn't deny yourself an opportunity because someone else faced some challenges. If you don't buy the property, you can bet another investor will. They will thank you each and every month the rent check rolls in.

5. **Can I borrow money on one property from two different banks? Will the second bank pull my credit and find a loan I didn't list on my financial statement?**

Sure, just remember to write your family every month from jail. Trying to play banks against one another is always a bad idea. Whenever you fill out an application with a traditional bank, you will have to list your assets and liabilities. If you don't, you may have committed a little thing prosecutors and judges like to call bank fraud, and you may be roused from your warm bed and dragged into a cold jail cell.

Any lender will run a credit check on you. It will also report its lien to credit agencies to protect their interests. Savvy investors always use the highest level of integrity, and that means being as open and honest as possible on loan applications. If you don't, at the least, your bank will find out and you will fracture the relationship you have built with them. At the worst, you will get an extended invitation to the Grey Bar Hotel.

6. I was at one of my properties making sure a repair had been completed when I saw drugs on the living room table. Is this a problem? Should I do anything?

Awesome. Call the tenant, fire up the bong, and get your party on. Maybe he can refer some of his friends to you and you can rent out all of your properties to his druggie buddies.

Start by taking a picture with your cell phone or the digital camera you keep in your truck. Then call the police, and start eviction proceedings as quickly as possible. People who do drugs will bring you nothing but trouble and may cause you to lose the empire it has taken you years to build. You may get a call in the middle of the night and learn that the police have kicked in the front door to arrest the tenant for dealing drugs. Maybe you will turn on the TV and see a breaking news story about a meth lab in a residential neighborhood that exploded. When you look closer, you realize that it's one of your properties and you see all of your hard work and money turning into smoke. Walter White may be a compelling television character, but you don't want him renting from you.

7. How do I prepare for the winter and prevent my pipes from freezing and bursting?

Water damage is one of the worst things that can happen to your properties. One of the few things that can be worse is water that finds its way onto your property and freezes. If you own property in an area prone to freezing, start by reminding tenants to leave faucets dripping when the weather turns cold. You can also insulate any exposed pipes fairly inexpensively. Foam pipe insulation can be bought fairly cheaply from any home improvement store. If you are going to do it, consider buying at least one-inch foam. It doesn't cost much more than smaller insulation and offers more protection.

Another option would be to wrap the pipes in electric pipe tape. It's more expensive, and the tenants need to know the tape will increase their electric bills when the weather turns cold.

Crunch your numbers and see what makes the most sense for you. But don't sit around and wait for snow to fall before you do anything. You won't have a Merry Christmas if the Grinch brings you a sack of busted pipes.

8. **What is a revocable trust?**

You should bring this up with your attorney as soon as you can. Hopefully, you did this before you bought your first property. The simple version is that a revocable trust is an estate-planning tool that allows you to control where your assets go in the event you kick the bucket. The word "revocable" means that the trust can be modified, and the property owned by the trust can be returned to you. The main advantage may be that property owned by a trust is automatically transferred to the beneficiary, and there is no need to have the estate probated. Your attorney can tell you if placing your company or properties in a revocable trust is a smart move for you, and you should consult him soon if you have not already done so.

9. **What does "pierce the corporate veil" mean?**

No, this does not have anything to do with wedding rituals at some bizarre cult. One of the main benefits of creating a corporation is shielding yourself from legal liability. If someone is injured on property owned by your corporation, the corporation would normally get sued and not you. However, under certain circumstances courts can ignore the corporate structure and hold officers and shareholders of the corporation liable for the company's debt. These circumstances vary from state to state, so you will need to consult with your attorney to see what applies in your area.

Here are a few of the reasons that can cause the corporate veil to be pierced:

If you use the corporation to commit fraud.

If you establish a corporation and plan to buy thousands of dollars' worth of material from a home supply store with no intention of paying for them, a judge might allow the corporate officers or shareholders to be held individually liable.

You don't follow the rules regarding formalities every corporation must follow.

These might include not having annual meetings or failing to pay annual corporate dues to the state.

The important thing to remember is that a corporation is a great structure to build your empire, but just because you have a corporation doesn't mean you will always be protected in every circumstance. Be sure to visit with the attorney on your team to make sure you are doing what you need to do to protect yourself.

10. How many properties do I need to own to be financially independent and never have to work again?

I wish there were some magic number. Knowing this answer would make my life so much easier. If I knew I only had to own twenty, thirty, or fifty properties to make my dreams come true I would get to that number, kick back, and wait for the cash to roll in. But there is no set number. It depends on a lot of factors. How much is your dream going to cost?

If you desire to live in a mansion in Beverly Hills or Paris, you're going to need more monthly cash flow than if your dream is to own a small farm in Texas. If your dream is to travel the world and stay in five-star hotels you will need to have more cash flow than you would need if your goal is to stay at home and watch TV.

The real issue isn't the number of properties you own. The number that matters is your cash flow. Having twenty properties doesn't necessarily mean you will make twice as much money than if you only owned ten. The key is owning the right houses, doing your due diligence so that the numbers crunch, and that you get the return on your investments you need to make your dreams come true.

11. How do I calculate my net worth?

Net worth is the value of all the things you own minus the total amount of what you owe on them. If you own $1,000,000 worth of property and have loans worth $500,000 on them, your net worth is $500,000 (plus the value of any other property you have, such as cash or stocks).

Keep in mind that net worth really only takes into account the present value of things. Last year, my business really took off. I nearly doubled the number of properties I owned. On paper, I'm now worth over $1,000,000. But the properties are leveraged with other people's money, so my actual worth is much less than that. However, in a few years, when I begin paying off the loans my net worth is going to increase, and I will live like a rock star. At the same time, the properties will, almost always, be appreciating and this will help my net worth increase as well. The point is to look at the value of your property over the long haul. Don't treat it as a snapshot that will never change. You are making a full-length, major motion picture.

12. Should I let a tenant have a waterbed in my rental? Waterbed? Do they still make those?

I thought they quit manufacturing those about 1980.

You would think this would be a simple question. A landlord should have the right to restrict people from bringing things into their property if they can cause damage. When I hear the word waterbed, the first thing I see is the mattress springing a leak and all that water leaking into my carpet and floors. Water damage sucks and can destroy your property quickly! I would never let anyone bring a waterbed into one of my properties if I could legally stop them.

But in some states you cannot refuse people the right to own a waterbed. You need to check with your legal professional before you tell prospective tenants they cannot bring their waterbeds with them. If you are required to allow people to use waterbeds (or just decide to do so out of the goodness of your heart), I would charge the maximum security deposit the law allows. This varies by state, and some even have specific laws that define how much of a deposit you can charge tenants who have waterbeds. Know your rights and responsibilities before you make any decisions about renting to people who want to swim while they sleep.

13. How do I prequalify a prospective tenant?

This is the Holy Grail all investors are trying to find. If you get the right people into your properties, your life will be so simple. They will pay their rent on time, not throw wild parties, and if they move out the building will be cleaner than the day they moved in.

The most important thing to do is your due diligence. Find out as much as you can about your tenants before they move in. Once you give them the keys, you may have a hard time getting them out if they turn out to be losers. Make every tenant complete a written application and verify every detail on it. Run a credit report, and you will see what their track record is with paying their bills. The more you know about prospective tenants the better you will be at finding good ones.

You're going to get burned. It's part of the learning process. It's not easy and nobody likes it, but use those failures as an opportunity to learn and improve.

14. **How often should I check on my rental properties?**

Ideally, you should check every day. You need to know if any problems have come up, and the sooner you know about them the better. But every day is not a realistic option, especially as you own more and more properties. You should never go a month without inspecting every one of your properties, even if it is only a drive-by to make sure everything is fine. Your rental agreement should include a term that gives you permission to enter the property and inspect it with notice. If you have long-term tenants who haven't caused you any trouble you might consider not inspecting every month, but that should be done on a case-by-case basis and only with people who have proven themselves to be trustworthy.

15. **How do I evict a tenant?**

You really don't need to know this information because tenants will never give you any trouble. Everyone who signs a lease will pay on time, leave the place in better shape than the day he moved in, and will never have any parties that disturb the neighbors. You will become best friends with all your tenants, and you will exchange Christmas cards every year. If you believe any of that, put this book down and seek professional help because you have no grasp on reality.

You will have to evict people when you are a real estate investor. There is no way around it. Even when you do as much due diligence as possible, people will let you down on accident, and some of them will screw you over. Eviction can be a complicated process, and if you don't do it the way the law requires it in your state, you may live to regret it. In worst-case scenarios, you may have to pay fines or penalties if you try to evict your client but don't do it the right way. Before you buy your first property, meet with your attorney. One of the items on your checklist should deal with evictions and how to properly do them. Be proactive. Recognize that evictions are part of the cost of doing business when you are building an empire, and don't take it personally when it happens.

But personally handling evictions shouldn't be part of your long-term plan to build an empire. Hire an eviction attorney to handle the process for you. I pay $150 plus filing fees for my evictions, and it is a great investment. I don't have to waste time in court, and I can spend my time looking for great properties.

16. Am I required to provide smoke detectors?

Almost half of the states require rental properties to have smoke detectors, and some also require carbon monoxide detectors. Consult with your attorney, and make sure that your properties are up to code. Remember that smoke and carbon monoxide detectors will require routine maintenance, and that means money out of your pocket. Be sure to crunch the numbers and make sure you are charging enough rent to make the numbers work.

You will need to include a routine inspection schedule. You need to make sure every detector is working, and when they aren't you will need to repair or replace them. If you don't and, God forbid, something happens, you could find yourself on the wrong end of a lawsuit.

I provide smoke detectors. They are less than ten dollars at home improvement stores, and in some places you can get them free at fire stations.

You might include an addendum to your leases to protect yourself from the fire marshal, and if you need them, we have sample forms on our website at www.savvylandlordbooks.com/resources.

17. The roof on my rental looks a little rough. Should I have a new one installed? Easy there, big shot. Do you have a money tree out back? If so, can you give me a few of the seeds?

I would like to have one of those myself. Roofs are expensive. The only time you should replace one is when it is damaged and cannot be repaired, or when it is so old that leaving it up might hurt your property.

Roofs will never look good. They sit under the sun for years at a time, and are exposed to wind, rain, and snow. If you replaced a roof every time it looked bad, you would make every roofing contractor in the state rich. Savvy landlords only replace roofs when they have to and get the best deal they can with their roofing contractors.

18. My insurance agent suggested I replace the roof on one of my properties. Do I have to? How strong of suggestion was it? Did it happen after a major windstorm blew through the area or after there was a fire in the garage at one of your properties?

One of the best things you can do is to build a long-term relationship with your insurance agent, and you will know when he is making idle conversation and when he is telling you something needs to be done. If he starts talking about adjusters or starts sending you things in writing, you should get your roofer on the phone immediately.

When you own enough properties, you will have a sense of when things on your property need to be repaired or replaced. You will be able to look at a roof and know when it needs to be replaced.

If push comes to shove, pull out the mortgage and see whose name is on it. You are in control, not your insurance agent.

19. When should I raise the rent? How often can I do that?

Being an investor is a business. It's about making money, and the more of it the better. You should raise the rent as often as you can. The only times you could never raise the rent is when a tenant has a signed lease or if the property is subject to rent control. If you own property in an area that is growing and desirable, you may be able to raise the rent every time the lease expires.

But you don't want to price yourself out of the market. You need to understand what your property is worth. If similar properties in the area are renting for $750 a month, and you list yours at $1100, you may wait a while before anyone is willing to pay you. The truth is that you will never be able to charge more than the market will bear, because people won't rent from you if you charge more than what your property is worth. Understand your market, and know when other investors are raising their rates. Then you will know when it's time to raise yours.

Not raising your rents can be a problem. I learned the hard way that if your rents are not market value it looks bad to your bank and your ratios will be off. Don't let this happen to you.

20. Do I really have to pass out a lead-based paint pamphlet?

If you are renting property that was built before 1978, you will need to hand potential renters a lead-based paint pamphlet. Houses built before that year may have lead-based paint, which may cause illness or birth defects. Not distributing the pamphlet is a serious issue (it's a federal offense and could be illegal under state law as well), and renters need the information to make an informed decision before signing a lease. The government takes it seriously, and if you don't distribute the pamphlet you can be assessed fines.

21. What are the dangers of not using a move-in sheet?

A move-in sheet is a simple piece of paper that has a list of everything you need to check when a client moves in, such as the condition of the carpet or floors and the paint on the walls. Use one with every property you own for every tenant. You inspect each area of the house with your tenants before they move in, and they sign the sheet agreeing that the property is in the condition you describe. When the tenant moves out, you walk through the house with him and compare the condition of the house with the check-in sheet. If there is any damage, you'll have all the proof you need with the move-in sheet and a few photos taken on your phone or the digital camera you keep in your truck.

If you don't use one with each tenant you should close your office and find another career. Not having a move-in sheet means that you won't be able to prove the condition of the property when the tenant moved in, and that may mean you won't be able to keep his security deposit or sue him for the cost of the repairs if he damages your investment. A move-in sheet and a few digital pictures won't cost more than a nickel, and it's some of the cheapest insurance you will ever have.

22. **What is a debt ratio?**

A debt ratio is a financial term, and is one of the most important factors lenders will use to determine if you get a loan. Debt ratio is calculated by dividing the amount of debt in your portfolio by the value of your assets. If your portfolio is worth $1,000,000 but is secured by $250,000 in loans, your debt ratio is 25 percent. If it is secured by $500,000 in loans, your debt ration is 50 percent. You get the idea.

The lower the percentage, the better. If you have a high debt ratio, you may be perceived as a high risk loan and your application may be denied or you may be charged a higher interest rate. You should always have a general idea of what your debt ratio is and make sure you manage your debt in the way that helps you grow your portfolio as quickly as possible.

23. **What are the differences between the three basic business structures: sole proprietor, corporation, and partnership?**

Choosing the right business structure for your situation is important, and before you decide which one is right for you consult your accountant and attorney.

A sole proprietor is a fancy way of saying that the business is being run by an individual. It's the lowest level of legal protection, and offers you virtually no protection from lawsuits. I don't know any savvy investors who operate as a sole proprietor.

A corporation is a business structure that operates like a person. It is able to own property and incur debt and has its own tax ID number. If you establish and operate a corporation properly, it can offer the best protections for most investors.

A partnership is a group of individuals who come together to form a business. Each partner shares in the profits according to his ownership percentage and is liable for debts in the same percentage. If there are four partners and they have equal shares in the partnership, they each receive 25 percent of the profits and must pay 25 percent of any liabilities. If you structure your business as a partnership, make sure that you have a written agreement that spells out how much each partner owns and what the liabilities are. You also need to be clear about what happens if the partnership is dissolved. If things don't work out everyone needs to have an understanding of what their rights and obligations are.

24. How much money can I borrow to build my empire?

As much as possible. There is no set limit on how much money you can borrow. But banks won't lend you more than they think you can repay. If you look like a good risk and can demonstrate the ability to repay it, you could borrow millions from the right bank. One of the most important concepts of real estate investing is to use other people's money as much as possible. Borrowing money to build your empire is a good thing. It allows you to leverage your assets and gives you some awesome tax deductions. Borrow as much as you can afford and as much as the bank will loan you.

25. Can I borrow against my retirement account?

Yes, but only some retirement accounts qualify for this, such as a self-directed IRA. Borrowing against your retirement account can be a good way to build your empire, and you may even get a favorable interest rate by doing so. But you should keep a few things in mind. It's always better to borrow other people's money. Don't put your retirement account in jeopardy by borrowing against it if you can avoid it.

Another issue to keep in mind is that depending on how you repay the account your future balance may be impacted. Always consult your tax professional before taking any money out of a retirement account.

26. How do I determine the fair market rental value of my property? Should I use Zillow or eppraisal, or an average of the two?

This is a wise question. You have to understand the value of your properties to grow your empire as quickly as you can. In fact, you have to understand the value of properties before you buy them. If you don't, you may pay too much, the numbers will never add up, and it will take years for you to make money. If you don't understand the value of your properties when it is time to determine how much to charge for rent, one of two things will happen. You will not charge enough, which means you are giving away money. Or you will charge too much, which means prospective tenants will rent from another landlord, and you will be stuck covering the holding costs out of your pocket.

You can never have too much information to determine the true value of your properties. Use Zillow, eppraisal, and look in the newspaper to see what other landlords are charging for similar properties near yours. Pull comps from a real estate agent if you can. Use a Magic 8 Ball if you think it will help. Look at as many sources as you can to make sure you don't leave money on the table.

27. Do I need to order a mortgage inspection?

A mortgage inspection (which is also called a plot plan) ensures the property you are buying is free of any encroachments and isn't sitting in the middle of a flood plain. Many lenders will require you to obtain a mortgage inspection before they loan you money. They want to protect their investment and to make sure the house you are buying isn't going to be swept away the next time it rains. In my area, mortgage inspections cost about $140, and I negotiate the cost with the seller. If the seller is willing to pick up the expense, it saves you a lot of money in the long haul.

28. I don't connect with the people at my local real estate group. Should I start my own investment club?

You don't think people like you and now you want to go play somewhere else? Starting your investment group is a bad idea for a lot of reasons. How much credibility do you have? If you are new to the investing game, what do you bring to the table to make people want to join your club?

If people don't think you know what you are doing you may be the only person at your club's meetings.

Why don't people connect with you? Do you have trouble relating to people in other situations? Maybe this would be a good learning opportunity for you to improve your interpersonal skills. At the very least you could understand that not everyone is going to like you. It's a fact of life. But that shouldn't prevent you from being able to attend meetings with other investors and learning as much as you can from them, even if you are not great friends.

If you need more information than you are receiving at your REIA and still want to start your own club, start small. Have lunch with three other investors and call it a landlord's lunch. If that goes well, invite others into the group.

29. I own ten properties and I am not wealthy yet. Becoming rich is taking too long. Should I start flipping properties? Impatient much?

I bet you were one of those kids who tried to find where his parents hid the Christmas toys and unwrapped them before they were under the tree. Quit thinking short-term and focus on the future.

Owning and managing properties as an investor is a fundamentally different business model than flipping properties. When you flip properties, you buy them (hopefully undervalued), hold them for a short period of time, maybe make a few improvements, and then sell them at a profit. It is not a way to build long-term wealth. Flipping is great if you need cash now and aren't worried about the future.

Owning properties as an investor is a long-term strategy to build substantial wealth. Once you learn the rules of the game, it will provide you with income for decades. It's one of the best ways to live a lifestyle most people only dream of and to provide for your family.

30. I just received my property tax bill and it's outrageous. It's assessed at $80,000, but I only paid $35,000 for it. How can I force the assessor to come to reality?

In a perfect world, every property would be assessed at the correct value, or, even better, they would be undervalued. But that doesn't happen often. If it does, keep your mouth shut or the assessor will knock on your door and try to shake some extra cash out of your pockets.

Every jurisdiction has a method for property owners to dispute assessments. It may include filing paperwork with the city or county and then appearing in person to make your argument. You may even have the right to appeal to a judge.

You can avoid this problem by doing your due diligence and knowing the last assessed value on the property. That should be a matter of record, and that information will prevent you from getting sticker shock when the tax bill arrives in the mail next year. Many places have limits on the amount property values can increase each year, and that offers some protection. But the best defense is information, such as knowing what the property is worth and what your rights are if assessments are out of line.

Every sale of property triggers an assessment to be performed, and you should be prepared for your taxes to increase on new properties.

31. **My LLC is in my name. Should I change that?**

Deciding which entity owns your limited liability corporation (LLC) can have serious implications, on issues such as tax liability or estate planning. How you should structure ownership of your company is a serious decision and is something you need to discuss with your attorney and accountant. Make sure you get the maximum advantages our tax code has to offer and that your company structure and how it is owned give you the best chance for success. Do it right from the start. If something happens, you may not get a second chance. Liability and how to protect yourself from it should be priorities from the day you start investing.

32. **I just applied for a loan. What's the difference between being pre-qualified and pre-approved?**

This is the type of legal mumbo-jumbo and hair-splitting that makes lawyers drool. It makes them think of expensive vacations and new leather shoes. Pre-qualified doesn't mean much to investors. It essentially means you are in a pool of potential applicants, and that the lender would review your application. It doesn't mean anything beyond that.

Pre-approved, however, is gold to investors. It means that the lender has committed funds to you. All you have to do is to submit your application, they will make sure the paperwork is in order, and a check will follow. If you stumble across a bank that is generously handing out pre-approved loans, please ask them to put my name and address on their mailing list. I have my eyes on a few more properties and would love to use their money to get the deals done.

33. My loan officer said my loan is approved, but he has to present my loan application to the loan committee or the board of directors. Is that normal?

Yes. As strange as it may seem, banks don't give their loan officers keys to their vaults. Loan officers don't have the power to write you a check on the spot. They have to submit your application to the loan committee for final approval. However, if a loan officer tells you your loan has been approved, it's a safe bet the committee will agree. Loan officers have a sense of which loans will be approved and which will be denied, and they don't want to submit applications they know their bosses will reject. But don't write checks until the funds are in the bank.

34. An investor suggested we do the closing at his office. He said there was no need to use a title company. What are the advantages of not using a title company?

The main advantage of not using a title company is that it makes it much easier to lose your money. In the blink of an eye, with no effort at all, you can wave your empire goodbye.

Not using a title company is a foolish mistake. Title companies research the chain of title on your properties and make sure there are no encumbrances. Using a title company gives you the protection of knowing that you have clear title to the properties you bought with your hard-earned or (borrowed) money.

If there is ever a dispute to the title, the title company will have to defend your right to the property. If you don't use a title company, you will have to foot the bill and hire an attorney to fight for you. As you know, attorney fees add up quickly (they never miss the chance to send you a bill). A title search will only cost a few hundred dollars at most and is a bargain compared to what most attorneys will charge. And don't forget to purchase title insurance. It's another cheap way to protect your company.

35. **Someone at my local real estate investors' club said he negotiated his mortgage rate. Can you do that?**

Yes. If you learn nothing else from this book, remember that virtually everything can be negotiated. This is especially true when you own multiple properties. I add the word "virtually" because property taxes can't be negotiated, but there aren't many other things that can't be. Banks will negotiate mortgage fees for investors who have been customers of the bank for a long time and for investors who own multiple properties. Even if you are not the bank's largest customer, there are simple things you can do to negotiate a lower interest rate. Pull a copy of your credit report, and take care of any blips or problems. You are entitled to one free credit report per year from each of the three major credit agencies, and that means you can get one every four months. You should also consider creditkarma.com.

Make your payments on time to your bank, and do whatever you can to develop rapport and open communication with them. Those relationships will come into play when you apply for a loan or ask for a lower interest rate.

You should also compare rates offered by different banks from time to time. I don't recommend jumping to another lender every time you see a lower rate, but knowing you have options gives you leverage when you apply for a loan or want to reduce your mortgage rate.

Negotiate on as many things as you can. You can negotiate with plumbers, electricians, and even with the home improvement stores where you buy your supplies. Negotiate with the laborers who paint your walls. The more properties you own, the more leverage you will have. Vendors will be willing to negotiate on one property if they think they can get more or all of your business. If you own ten properties and save $100 per year on each of them, you earned $1,000. That's not bad, but let's say you own forty properties and you save $200 per year by being a shrewd negotiator. That's $8,000 in your account at the end of the year.

36. **What is a deed of trust?**

Some people think it is something you do for people you have faith in. A deed of trust is a legal term for a method of securing property for a loan. In some states, deeds of trusts are used instead of mortgage liens. If a deed of trust is used, there are three parties to the transaction: the borrower, the lender, and a trustee. When the loan is made, the borrower transfers title to the property to the trustee by means of a deed of trust. The borrower still has possession and the right to use the property, but the lender is named as the beneficiary of the trust. If anything happens to the buyer or he fails to make payments on time, the lender owns the property. The trust is set up so that when the borrower pays off the loan, the trust expires and he owns the property outright. Check with your attorney to see if you are required to use a deed of trust or if it would be an advantage for you to do so. If you deal with many properties sold "subject to," you will encounter many deeds of trust.

37. **How do I know we are in an up market or down market?**

If you find out a sure fire way of knowing this, please send the information to me. I will split my profits with you 60/40 (but if you are a savvy investor you know not to take my first offer and will negotiate me up to at least 50/50).

The best ways to know if we are in an up or down market are experience (the more deals you do, the more you will understand the market) and by talking with people in the real estate industry. Members of your real estate investors' club and your banker can tell you about their deals and what they are doing. That information is free, and you need to take advantage of it.

When the market is up, people are paying for property and everyone is trying to be an investor. One great indicator is the attendance at your REIA club. If the attendance has been sixty members and it suddenly balloons to 125 or if more than 20 percent of the people there are newbies, the market is up. A more scientific method would be to ask your real estate agent for statistics. How many properties are selling? What is the average number of days properties are listed before they sell?

You also need to understand what to do during up and down markets. In down markets, property values may be lower and it may be a great time to buy. But you may be forced to lower your rents. When the market is up, property values may be too high to find any deals that fit your portfolio, but you may be able to raise rents on properties when leases expire. With experience, you will know how to maximize up and down markets to grow your empire.

38. Can a bank call up a loan anytime?

No. Banks can only call up loans under circumstances outlined in mortgage agreements. The purpose of the contract is to give both parties certainty and security. The lender knows when he is going to be paid and has rights if the borrower doesn't live up to his end of the deal. The borrower receives the money he needs and has ownership in the property as long as he pays on time.

Carefully review each and every mortgage contract before you sign it. Just because the last five mortgages you signed didn't include an escalation clause (the clause that allows the bank to call up your note) doesn't mean there won't be one in the future.

Even if there is an escalation clause in your mortgage, these thoughts should give you some peace of mind. Banks don't want to own property. If they did, they would go out and buy them. Plus, owning too much property affects their debt to asset ratio, and that looks bad to bank examiners.

39. What is a balloon loan and how does it work?

This has nothing to do with paying for a child's birthday party. A balloon loan is unlike a conventional loan, which is very straightforward, where the lender agrees to loan a certain amount of money and the borrower pays it back by making a set payment each month. In the balloon agreement, the payments are smaller each month, but at the end of the loan the borrower is required to pay back a large portion of the balance in one lump sum.

So, although the monthly payments in a balloon agreement are lower than the monthly payments in a conventional loan, the borrower has be prepared to pay off the outstanding balance at the end of the loan in one payment.

Under the right circumstances for some borrowers, balloon payments can work, but I prefer conventional loans. I want to know what I owe each month and I don't want the headache of having to come up with large payments in addition to meeting my loan payments, salaries, and maintenance.

Most banks will renew loans with balloon payments. They don't want people to pay off mortgages. They need borrowers in debt so they can charge interest and make money. The main reason banks offer balloon payments is to protect themselves against sudden increases in the prime interest rate. It costs banks to borrow money (usually about 2 percent), and when they loan it to you at 6 or 7 percent they keep the difference as profit.

40. Why do commercial lenders selling on second markets structure loans amortized over fifteen or thirty years with 3- or 5-year balloons?

Money. When you ask a question about real estate investing, the answer almost always comes down to cold, hard cash. The kind that buys you time on the beach and sends your kids to college. By amortizing the loan over a longer period of time, lenders generally offer lower interest rates. That means a lower monthly payment for the borrower, but the kicker is a higher balloon payment. Lenders are going to make their money somewhere, and if they can't earn it by charging a high interest rate they will increase the size of the balloon payment. It protects them if they can't service it on the local market.

41. One of my tenants wants to pay for someone to pour a new driveway. What are the pros and cons?

I'm all for tenants using their money to increase the value of my properties. If you know of any prospective tenants who want to paint a few places for free, please send them my way.

But as good as it sounds, it's not always wise to let tenants maintain property. Are they going to expect an offset on their rent? If so, that needs to be discussed in advance and the agreement needs to be in writing. Will they use professionals who will do a good job or will it be their buddy who has never poured a new driveway? You don't want to be stuck with the bill if someone else does a lousy job and you have to rip it out and start over. The worst possibility, however, is that a contractor will put a lien on your property if he isn't paid. The title to the property would be clouded, when you didn't even hire someone to do the job.

Savvy landlords don't let tenants work on their properties. The job of a tenant is to pay rent on time. The job of a landlord is to maintain the property. You should never do a tenant's job, and he should never do yours.

42. In your other books you say you never hire inspectors. Would you ever make an exception to this rule?

Almost never, and if I did I would require the seller to pay for it if possible. Some lenders require inspections, and if it is a deal breaker I will hire an inspector to get the deal done. When you gain experience as an investor, you won't feel the need to hire an inspector on every property. You will be able to walk through a property, see what needs to be done, and have a good sense of what that will cost. Even if you are not great with numbers, you will be able to crunch the numbers without hiring an inspector. That will save you thousands of dollars as you build your empire. If you are new and getting a deal on a property, save the $400 or use it as leverage during your negotiations.

43. **I have seen a lot of houses that have more than one layer of roof on them. Should I add an additional layer to the roofs on my properties?**

Sounds great. Add another layer of flooring and paint the walls three or four times while you are at it.

Making a roof thicker is a bad idea. The sheer weight of multiple layers of roofing shingles can cause stress on the framing of a roof and could cause truss's or rafters, to bow and/or break, you are less likely to see hail damage, it does not allow you to update the flashing when needed and multiple layers of roofing can hold heat and prematurely age. Spend the money to tear off the old shingles. Actually, the only time you should work on a roof is when it is damaged or old and needs to be replaced. If you have the time, please contact the owner of a house where the roof has more than one layer. Give him my name and number so I can talk to him about why he does this and how he has money to burn.

On a more practical and serious note, you may not qualify for some insurance policies if your property has more than one roof.

44. **Why is cash flow so high on low-income properties?**

Do not confuse low-income with low profit. The right low-income property can be a goldmine. Low-income properties are subsidized with tax dollars, and people who don't earn high incomes can apply for government assistance with their rent. They pay a portion of the rent based on their income, and the government pays the rest.

Landlords have to apply and be approved to be part of programs that qualify for low-income housing, but the program offers a dependable source of income. Owning low-income properties can be a great way to build your portfolio and your empire.

45. I heard someone talking about real estate cycles. What does that mean, and can I use that to my advantage as an investor?

Every type of investment goes through cycles. The stock market has highs and lows, the price of gold goes up and down, and the value of real estate fluctuates. You can and should use this to your advantage as an investor. Ideally, you want to buy real estate in the down cycle, when the price has fallen as low as it will go. You want to avoid buying when it is high. If you buy at the right time, the numbers will crunch in your favor. If you buy at the wrong time, it may take years to make money. Do your due diligence, know when to buy, and you will be on the way to making a comfortable living as an investor. When you buy, buy for cash flow and not appreciation, and you should be good.

46. What does competition look like as an investor?

After I read this question, I turned on my TV and tuned it to the Discovery Channel. I watched a show about a lion in Africa. He was fighting hyenas for the leg of a zebra killed by a lioness in his pride. The lion looked happy as he chewed on that leg, and the hyenas scurried away, their bones sticking through their skin.

Get the idea? Being an investor is challenging. You have to hunt every day, and you have to understand that there will be other lions and hyenas chasing the same prey as you. When you win, and get to eat under the warm sun, you feel great. When you lose, you have to sulk away and wonder what happened. Win or lose, you have to always be on the prowl and start hunting for the next deal. Some days you are the lion, and some days you are a hyena. Wake up every day ready to hunt and great things will happen.

47. **One of the landlords I know said his property manager charged him a "trip fee." What does that mean?**

It means your friend is probably overpaying his property manager. Property managers are usually paid a percentage of the rent they collect. This gives then an incentive to keep the units full and to make sure rent is paid on time. Some are allowed to live in one of the units in exchange for their services, and some are paid by a combination of both.

Some property managers will bill you if they have to visit a property to inspect it or to check on tenant complaints. Suppose a tenant calls the property manager because the hot water heater isn't working. The manager goes out to the property and determines you need to install a new water heater. As soon as she gets back to the office, she sends you a bill for the trip. That is a trip fee.

Regardless of how you pay your property manager, make sure your agreement is in writing and that you take into account things such as property inspections and how the manager is to be paid. You don't want to lose a good manager because you didn't take the time to draft a decent agreement and read it.

You should also consider including a clause that outlines how the arrangement can be terminated. You don't want to be stuck with a lousy property manager any longer than you have to be. If the process of letting someone go is spelled out in writing before you hire him it will make your life much easier. Never, ever forget that you are in control. It is your asset, and you have the power to say "yes" or "no" when it comes to spending your money.

48. **A landlord told me under his business model he makes a lot of money on fees. What fees can I charge my tenants?**

Charge as many fees as you legally can and that your tenants will tolerate. You are in business to make money, and you shouldn't let opportunities pass you by. Before you start charging tenants for sunshine and fresh air, make sure to consult with your attorney and confirm what is legal in your area. What landlords can charge varies from place to place, and you don't want pay a big fine for something you could have avoided. It will take years of new key fees to cover those fines.

Also, keep in mind that people get tired of paying fees. You don't like it when your bank charges you for every tiny transaction, do you? Your tenants won't either, and if you go crazy with charges they may move down the street to a house owned by one of your buddies. Don't give up months of rent to collect a few dollars in fees.

49. Should I know the crime rate for an area where I plan to buy investment property?

You should know as much as possible about every area where you own property. You should know where the local schools are so that you can discuss them with prospective tenants with children. You should know where the nearest police station and fire station are. And you should also know about the crime rate in the area. Do you want to spend tens of thousands of dollars to own and rent units next to a crack house? What happens if a meth lab in the house across the street blows up and sets your property on fire?

If you know the area has a high crime rate, potential tenants will too. And that may make it difficult or impossible to rent the property to the kind of people you want to live in your units.

If you know what the crime rate in an area is, you probably don't have to share that information with prospective tenants. If you are trying to rent one of the houses you own in a less than desirable part of town, I wouldn't start the sales pitch with something like, "You're going to love this neighborhood if you are a crack addict. Just three doors down, you can buy rocks all night long. It's a really exciting place to live because there have been five shootings in the last three months."

50. **What is the capitalization of income?**

Investors have to use a simple but effective way of determining the true value of property. Capitalization of income is a method that allows them to compare the relative value of investments regardless of how much money they are paying. Just because a property is more expensive than another doesn't mean it's a better investment.

To determine the capitalization of income, determine how much it would cost to buy the property. If it has sold recently, that should be easy. Suppose it is a duplex that sold last year for $40,000.

Now determine the net revenue for the property for a year (income after expenses). Assume that you rent each duplex for $800 a month, but you have $100 in monthly expenses. You net $700 a month per unit, or $16,800 per year. You divide the yearly net by the value of the property. In this case, 16,800/40,000, which equals 0.42. The higher the number, the better the investment.

51. **What is the difference between ARV and policy value?**

Part of your job as an investor is to understand the basics of insurance. You have to speak the same language as your insurance agent. If you don't, you will be at the mercy of other people if one of your properties is destroyed. And you don't want to be in that position.

ARV stands for after repair value, and it is sometimes called after-rehab value. It is the fair market value of a property after any necessary improvements or repairs have been made. This policy ensures that the property is returned to the value it was before the damage. Policy value allows property to be repaired to the value it was at the time it was insured. If you buy the property and the insurance at the right time, using property value insurance can be a great way to build your portfolio. The key is that you want to buy the property when prices are high (which goes against what most savvy landlords do). If the value of the property decreases and is damaged, your policy will pay you the higher amount. But if you buy the house during a downturn in the market, the value will likely only increase. Your policy will be based on the lower value, and you will have to pay the difference. Before deciding on which type of insurance to buy, consult with your insurance agent and your accountant. It's an important decision and shouldn't be made lightly.

52. Should I self-insure my properties?

Self-insurance can be appealing. The idea is that instead of making monthly insurance payments, investors set aside a certain amount of money to cover any losses or damages to their property. When it is needed, they take money out of the account and pay for the repairs out of pocket. Part of the appeal is that you are paying yourself instead of an insurance company. But don't rush over to your insurance agent's office and cancel your policies just yet. There are a few things to think about before you decide if self-insurance is right for you. One of the key issues is to decide how much money to set aside. How much risk do you have? If all of your properties were damaged in a tornado or fire could you afford to repair them?

If you own ten properties in the desert your risk may be very small compared to someone who owns 100 properties in the heart of Tornado Alley. You may also lose a substantial tax deduction by cancelling your insurance. Insurance is generally a valid tax deduction and giving it up may have serious tax implications. Don't make this decision without consulting with your insurance agent and accountant.

You should keep general liability insurance. You don't want to be writing checks every time someone says he slipped and hurt himself at one of your properties.53. What's a yellow letter? If you are going to grow an empire, you will have to market your properties for rent, and you will also have to seek out properties to buy. "Yellow letter" is a marketing tool that many investors use and may be an effective way for you to find new investment properties. The idea is that if you see a property you like, you send the owner a hand-written note on paper from a yellow legal pad, stating that you are interested in purchasing the property. The address on the envelope should be hand-written as well. The hand written note and envelope makes the "cold call" seem more personal, and the owner is more likely to open the letter. Savvy investors have a detailed marketing plan, and yellow letters can be an important part of that.

54. What is a probate sale? How does probate work?

Probate is easy to understand. All you have to do is graduate from college and law school, pass the bar examination, and spend five or ten years listening to probate hearings at the local courthouse. No problem, right?

Probate is one of the ways that property is passed from someone who dies to his heirs. It is tightly regulated, and the process varies from location to location. If a homeowner passes away and his house has not been placed in a trust, the house may be sold as part of the probate process. The funds from the sale of the house become part of the probate estate, and they are distributed according to state law.

Probate sales can be great places for investors to find new properties at low prices. Many properties wind up in probate sales because heirs of the property owner don't want to own the house or invest the time and money to rent it on their own. They want to sell it as quickly as possible. Keep your ear to the ground, and take the time to find probate sales. They can be a great way to build your portfolio.

55. How many properties should I own before I hire a property manager?

If you are serious about building an empire, you should be thinking about hiring a property manager before you buy your first property. But it won't make sense to hire one until your portfolio grows. Part of the learning curve in real estate investing involves knowing the business from the ground up, and that includes painting walls, tearing out fixtures, and crawling through attics to look at ductwork. If you haven't done any of that, you won't have the foundation you need to hire the right manager and make sure he is doing his job.

Something else to consider is whether or not you are investing full-time or whether you will be working another job until you own enough properties and can afford to quit. So the number of properties to own before hiring a manager depends on you and your circumstances. If you hire one too soon, you will deny yourself the opportunity to learn the ins and outs of property ownership. If you do it too late, you will work too hard and delay the growth of your empire.

56. **How do I kill mold?**

Mold. I hate that word. I hear it and all I can think of is money flying out of my pocket. The best way to kill mold is to prevent it. Inspect your properties on a regular basis, and make sure that your tenants are cleaning and maintaining them as they should. If you discover places where water is leaking into a property, repair it as quickly as you can.

If mold begins growing, you need to take action as quickly as you can. What you do will depend on the type of material the mold is growing on. Moldy sections of drywall may need to be cut out and replaced, but if the drywall has been primed and painted you may be able to remove the mold with a washcloth and some mold killing solution. Mold on wood can be treated in a similar fashion, and mold on tile or grout is easy to treat.

The takeaway is to understand that mold will destroy your property and eat your money. If it gets bad enough, mold can impact your tenants' health and you may be forced to pay a mold abatement company to remove it. Always keep a supply of mold killing solution on hand. It's available at all home improvement stores and it is cheap, so there is no excuse for not having some nearby. Mold will eventually happen on at least one of your properties, but stopping it early is cheap and easy.

Just to be on the safe side, I have my tenants sign a mold addendum to protect me.

57. What does it mean to farm an area?

Think about what farmers do. They find an empty plot of land, till the soil, plant seeds, water and nurture them, and wait for a harvest. You need to do the same to build your empire. "Farm an area" is a term for a marketing technique you should use. You find an area where you want to invest and develop a marketing plan that targets owners of properties in the area. The idea is to plant seeds by sending letters or cards letting them know you are interested. You nurture the seeds by following up with any prospects, and you harvest your crop when you find an owner willing to sell you a property at a price that makes sense. The key is to think long term. It may take more than one season to reap a harvest, but the results will be worth it.

58. Should I do preseason?

Doing a preseason or annual tune up is vital to keep your HVAC and water heaters in working order. Most HVAC companies will inspect and service heating and air conditioning systems for a nominal fee. They may check the coolant level, make sure the filters are clean, and find any small issues before they become major problems.

It's much cheaper to pay for annual service than it is to pay for a service call on a holiday weekend. Connect with a reputable HVAC company and let them check your systems on a regular basis.

59. I have a prospective tenant who looks like she would be a great tenant, but her house is being foreclosed. How should I handle this?

The unfortunate reality is that many people go through tough times and find themselves in homes they can no longer afford. Here are a few things to consider if you find yourself in this situation. Charge a higher deposit and first and last month's rent. If the tenant breaks the lease, this will help offset your costs.

Review the applicant's credit report with a fine-tooth comb, and then review it again. Has the applicant had other troubles? Did she have a history of paying bills on time before her circumstances changed? Be sure to look at the rest of her credit history and how she pays bills other than her mortgage.

Request a co-signor. Put someone else's name on the lease, and make sure he has great credit.

60. I was visiting one of my properties when the tenant pointed out the shiny new carport her neighbor installed. It's obvious she is dropping a hint. What should I do?

Absolutely nothing. Your job as an investor is to provide safe housing at a reasonable price. You don't have to install every new gadget or accessory that the neighbors have. Trying to keep up with the people who own property near all of your investments is a great way to go broke.

I might think about installing a carport for a long-term tenant as part of negotiations. If she agreed to sign a new lease for a year or two and the numbers crunched, for example. But I would never do it just because the tenant likes the way the one next door looks.

61. I watched a tenant's baby fall into a big hole that their dog dug in the yard. Who's responsible if the kid gets hurt?

Let's slow down here for a second. Please tell me that you helped the kid and didn't just sit in your truck wondering if you might have to pay a few hospital bills. You're not that heartless, are you?

It would be difficult to say if you would be liable or not in this situation. The laws vary from place to place and a lot of things would come into play. But that is not the point. Scenarios like this are perfect examples of why you need to make sure you have enough property insurance and that your business is structured to give you the most protection. If not, all it takes is one bored dog and a curious toddler and you could lose everything.

General liability insurance is worth every penny. If you don't have any, talk to your insurance agent and find a policy that works for you. If you already pay for GL, visit with your agent and make sure your policy has high enough limits to protect you and your company.

62. Will texting my tenants cause any privacy concerns?

I would tread lightly when you text tenants. I would not recommend texting anything that is not business related. Texting can be a valuable tool if used for the right things, such as confirming a repair or reminding them of a planned inspection. I would never text anything private or sensitive to a tenant. You never know who is reading your messages or who is holding the tenant's phone, and you don't want to get in the middle of someone else's personal issues. Some things, such as eviction notices, have to be done in writing and should never be done by text. It's important to remember that sending a text or an e-mail is not the same as talking to someone over the phone or in person, and that can lead to confusion. If you text tenants, make sure your messages are professional and to the point.

Text messages are a great tool to create a paper trail. They can protect you if there is a dispute or if you are accused of not taking care of needed repairs. If you can show the judge that you have been texting a tenant for days but she hasn't responded she won't have much of a response.

63. What is a self-directed IRA?

IRAs, individual retirement accounts, are plans that allow people to set aside money for retirement. Traditional IRAs limit where the account holder can invest his money. Generally, they are required to keep it in the stock market. But self-directed IRAs give the owner more control and more options as to where his money goes. The benefit to real estate investors is that funds from a self-directed IRA can be used to purchase real estate. You can build your empire in two ways. First, you set aside money for retirement and have a nest egg for the future. Second, you leverage those funds to buy property, which increases your cash flow and the value of your portfolio. If your advisors tell you a self-directed IRA helps you achieve your goals, take advantage of all they have to offer.

64. I heard some investors talk about private money. What is private money and is it worth it?

Private money means money that comes from private investors, as opposed to a bank or traditional lender. The return on investment can be high in real estate, but people have learned that owning property is not the only way to make money in the industry. People can also make money by taking it out of the stock market and loaning it to real estate investors. It pays a higher rate to the lenders, and the borrowers get relatively quick access to cash and don't have to go through all the headache and paperwork that most banks require.

65. My commercial bank suggested I use a line of credit. What can I do with a line of credit?

A line of credit can be a godsend for real estate investors. It is simply a pre-approved loan and is secured against your property. Once you have opened a line of credit, you have access to a set amount of funds and don't have to reapply. It's similar to a credit card, and you may even access the funds by using a card. Lines of credit allow you to use other people's money to build your empire, and as long as you use them responsibly they are a great way to do business.

Using a line of credit the right way can be a savvy means of doing business. You can purchase a new investment property with your line of credit, hold it for a few months with an interest only loan, and then get permanent financing. That will help you avoid up-front out-of-pocket fees, and closing can be much quicker because you don't have the hassle of applying for a new loan.

Talk to seasoned investors and they will probably talk your ears off about why this is a good idea. But remember to manage your credit wisely. A line of credit is like a loaded gun. Don't just randomly point and shoot. Before you use your line of credit, make sure you are in a position to refinance the property and that you have enough cash reserves if you need to make repairs.

66. I own a duplex. A single girl rents one side and a couple rents the other. The couple recently fought, and the single girl was scared. She called the police and left a message on my phone. What should I do?

If you own enough properties, this will eventually happen to you. You rent property to people, and people are not perfect. They have flaws and baggage, and they will bring their drama into your world. Some of this drama will be serious, and you may have to make difficult decisions.

It's not your job as an investor to get involved in the lives of your tenants. In fact, the more distant and strictly professional you can keep it, the better. But when a tenant puts others at risk or makes them uncomfortable, you have to consider all of your options. Whether or not you could evict someone on the statement described above would depend on many factors, including whether or not your tenant was arrested. What was the final outcome? Was there a conviction? Did someone go to the hospital? Was it a fist-fight or were words the only weapons used?

You have to decide what you feel comfortable with and whether or not the tenant's actions were so bad you need to evict him. Here are a few thoughts on what I would not do. Regardless of what was happening:

I would not put myself in a situation where I was trying to help or counsel a tenant.

I would not offer advice or personally try to correct the situation.

There are agencies and trained professionals who could intervene and make sure everyone was in a safe place. It may be difficult, but keep your focus on making good deals and finding the next property to buy.

67. **Is it a savvy move to open a credit account at my local home improvement store?**

Yes. As your empire grows, you will need access to other people's money. Borrowing money is a part of being a successful investor, and this includes having access to credit when you need to buy a new water heater or bathroom fixtures. You will also face setbacks and challenges as you build your business, and having a credit account ensures you will be able to get supplies when you need them, even when you face financial challenges.

But here is the warning. You have to use the credit responsibly. You can't max out the account and refuse to pay it. You can't use it to buy a bunch of shiny tools you don't need because they look cool. And you should never let your workers have access to the account, except for business necessities. Check your statement every month or login and check it more frequently on your computer.

68. **Do I have to pay an application fee to borrow money?**

I hate paying fees, I work hard for my money, and I don't want to give it away, but some lenders do charge application fees, especially hard money lenders and private money loans. Negotiate these, and eliminate them when you can.

Review each and every loan application and understand what fees you are paying. You don't want to look at your dwindling bank account and discover that you have been paying a ridiculous fee that you should have noticed months ago.

69. **I can't keep track of my tenants. How do I stay organized?**

Can't keep track of them? What does that mean? Did you lose them, and your money, on the way to the bank?

You don't have to be perfect to be a successful real estate investor, but you do need some basic organizational skills. At the very least you have to know what your strengths and weaknesses are and find ways to improve your deficits.

Laptops and smartphones have revolutionized the business world. Have trouble keeping track of who paid their rent and who didn't? There are several computer programs to help with that. Need to track expenses on each property? With a click of your mouse it can be done.

The only things you need to do are understand where you need help and find the right program or hire someone to do the work for you. Your ultimate goal should be to create a business that runs without you, and there is no better time to lay the groundwork than when you buy your first property. Two great websites for real estate investors are buildium.com and shoeboxed.com.

70. **I sent my handyman to a job, but he got arrested on his way to the site. He's calling from jail and wants me to post his bail. What should I do?**

The joys of finding good help. I wish I could tell you this story was fiction, but it's happened to more than one landlord. You have to decide what is right for you, but I wouldn't bail anyone out of jail. Savvy landlords keep their business and personal lives separate. Combining the two only creates problems, and I don't need more of those.

71. **Should I loan my worker money?**

Only if you never want to see either one of them again. Loaning money to workers is almost as bad as loaning money to family. It never ends well. Even if he pays you back on time, loaning money to a worker can strain your relationship and may even cost you a good employee. As tempting as it can be, keep your money in your pockets, and don't give it to employees.

72. **When should I add apartment buildings to my portfolio?**

Apartment buildings can be great investments, but they can be much more challenging than single-family properties. You should only add them to your portfolio when you understand the dynamics of multi-unit housing, when the numbers add up, and when owning them helps you meet your long-term goals. Buying apartments without understanding what you are getting into is a terrible idea. Buying one just because you think it would be cool or impress other investors is even worse. Stay focused on your goals, and only buy properties that make sense for you.

73. **I own seven properties. How much cash should I keep in the bank as a safety net?**

Congratulations. You are on your way to building an empire. Having a safety net is an important part of being a savvy landlord. You have to save enough cash to cover unexpected expenses and to stay solvent during slow periods. There will be times that challenge you financially, regardless of how big your portfolio is or how long you have been investing. You need to be prepared for that.

Ideally, you should set aside a minimum of three months of expenses for each property you own. If you set aside six months, you are a rock star. This is challenging, especially when you start your business, but having cash reserves will allow you to transition smoothly if something happens to one or all of your properties. With a cash reserve you will be able to restart with a minimum of stress and pain.

74. One of my tenants wants to buy the house he is renting from me, but he doesn't have any money. Should I sell it to him?

There is an expression for selling a house to a tenant who can't afford to pay for it. It's called giving away a house. What are you thinking?

Don't set yourself up for failure. If you know the guy doesn't have any money, don't waste your time by talking to him about buying the house. If he comes to you with a letter from his bank stating he is prequalified to buy the property and selling it makes sense in terms of your portfolio, then make the deal happen.

As you do more deals, you will develop a sense for which deals will work and which ones probably won't. Pass on the ones your gut tells you aren't going to work. It will save you a lot of trouble and headache in the long run, and you will have more money in the bank as well.

75. What are bandit signs? Do they work?

Bandit signs are small signs that investors place around town. They look like miniature billboards, and you may see them staked into yards or attached to telephone poles. Investors use them to let people know they are interested in buying houses and to let people know they have houses for rent.

As part of a bigger marketing campaign, bandit signs can be very effective. Make sure that the signs are well designed, that your contact information is clear and large enough to read as people go by, and that the signs convey a clear message. Are you buying or selling properties? The signs need to clearly state what your intentions are. And they have to be placed in the right areas, and you should have determined where those are before you bought your signs.

Spend a few bucks to make the signs look professional. You don't want your first impression to be that the only way you can advertise is with a crayon and a sheet of construction paper. If you want to be a serious player in the world of real estate investing, start acting like one.

76. What is section 8?

Section 8 is a government program that helps low income families find affordable housing. Property owners apply to the program, and their units have to be inspected and approved. Once that happens, Section 8 renters can rent homes. The renters pay a reduced amount for the property, and the government pays the difference between that and the monthly rent.

If you understand the program, Section 8 can be a great way to start or expand your empire. Many successful landlords have Section 8 properties, and if the program helps you achieve your dreams and build your portfolio you should take advantage of it.

77. What is a bridge loan?

Bridge loans are short-term loans that help investors make sure they have enough capital. They are typically used to help investors bridge-the-gap between when property is purchased or sold and when cash flow begins. There can be a gap between when you buy a new property and when it is ready to rent and create cash flow, and bridge loans can make that transition easier. They give investors more flexibility and allow them access to quick cash.

Do your due diligence before taking out bridge loans. The interest rates can be high, and you don't want to pay more than you have to.

78. What is transaction funding?

Think of transaction funding as micro-bridge loans. They are one-day loans and are designed with wholesalers and short sales in mind. Suppose you buy a property and before closing you find a buyer who will buy it from you at a profit. Technically, you only own the property for the brief period between when you buy the property and then sell it to the new buyer. Some states require that you have the property fully funded during that period, and transaction funding covers that.

79. What is micro-personal lending and how does it work?

Micro-personal lending, also called peer-to-peer lending, is a new niche in the lending market, and if you need quick cash you many want to explore it. Micro-lending typically deals with unsecured loans of $3,000 or less (some peer-to-peer lenders will loan as much as $35,000). Because the amounts are so small, they don't generate enough profit for most banks, and the market is not fully served. You can find multiple sites on the Internet that facilitate micro-personal loans between investors and borrowers.

Investors like micro-personal lending because the return can be substantial, much more that what they would receive in the stock market. Borrowers like it because the application process is more streamlined than with traditional lenders. Applications can be quickly approved or denied, and it can give them quick access to cash.

As with all credit, savvy investors should only use micro-personal lending if it helps build their portfolio and achieve their dreams. Use it responsibly, if you use it at all.

80. One of my tenants just checked out. He damaged the property, and his security deposit won't cover the repairs. What do I do?

Welcome to hell. A few quick questions before I answer this. What happened to your walk-through? Did you discover the damage before he left, or did you see it only after he was long gone? And when did the damage occur? Should it have been seen during your regular inspections of the property?

The short answer is that you will need to pay for the repairs out of your own pocket and then collect the costs over the security deposit from the tenant. You may have to sue him or hire a collection agency to get your money back. If you have read any of my other books, you know my opinion of suing people. It can be a waste of time, money, and energy. You should avoid it when you can, but there are times when you have to protect yourself and sue someone.

Having scheduled property inspections or a walk through can help you avoid being surprised by the damage a tenant leaves behind. It also gives you the opportunity to address a tenant's poor upkeep or misuse of your property before they "check-out".

At the very least, treat the experience as an opportunity to learn. A very expensive, frustrating, and emotionally-draining learning experience.

81. How much money does a prospective tenant need to make?

Learning to select the best tenants is one of the most important aspects of building your empire. When you learn to do that well, other things will start to fall in place. Even if a prospective tenant has sterling credit, a great rental history, and has a stable work history, you still need to crunch the numbers and make sure he can afford the rent. Set yourself up for success, and you will avoid problems down the road.

Some investors use ratios. They look at the tenant's income and see how what percentage of his monthly income the rent would be. If it is over a certain percentage (30 percent is a good rule), the tenant will not qualify. Other property owners use the "40-times Rule." They multiply the monthly rent by forty, and if the prospect's annual income is not at least that amount, they will not rent. For example, if the rent were $800 a month, the tenant would have to earn $32,000 per year. Some real estate markets are so competitive, landlords use a "50-times Rule."

Interestingly, if you use the 30 percent rule or the "40-times Rule" you will reach the same answer.

82. I have been told I can only get ten loans in my name. Is that true? How do I borrow more money?

Just a reminder. You should not be borrowing money in your name. It should be borrowed in your company's name.

Your company can only take out four FHA loans at one time, so the issue becomes how do you get more money. The best way to find new sources of credit is to get out and make it happen. Search out a local bank that has a history of loaning money to real estate investors. Call other investors and ask where they bank or if they know private lenders looking to invest. Money is there, but you may have to be creative in how you find it.

83. Should I hire a public adjuster to handle my insurance claim?

Public adjusters have been trained to read and interpret insurance policies, and they help people negotiate with insurance companies after a claim is filed.

Public adjusters serve a valuable service for homeowners and people who don't want to spend the time and energy needed to settle claims. But public adjustors cost money, and if you pay them that means profit is flying out of your pocket.

After you have been investing for a while, you will learn what needs to be repaired or replaced on a property. If one of your units is damaged, you can inspect it and know what needs to be taken care of. You will understand how much repairs will cost and if your adjuster has made a fair offer.

After you have negotiated a claim or two, you will be confident enough to know that you don't need to hire someone to do it for you. And you can sleep well, dreaming of all the money you saved.

That being said, there are times when it might be savvy to hire public adjusters. If the insurance company is lowballing you and you don't have the time or interest in dealing with the adjuster, it would be worth making a phone call.

Public adjusters can be especially helpful with larger claims. They are paid a percentage of the funds they collect, but they can earn that by getting higher returns. And they free up your time so that you can work on putting deals together.

84. What do underwriters do? What is the difference between in-house and outsourced underwriters?

Underwriters are the gatekeepers between you and your lender's money. After a lender has approved your application an underwriter will review your file with a fine-tooth comb. He will look under any rocks he finds. It is his job to verify every detail you provided and to find anything about you that you tried to hide or failed to mention. If an underwriter contacts you, respond as quickly as you can and give whatever information he asks for.

Underwriters generally look at three facets of you and your application. They are often called the three Cs: credit, capacity, and collateral.

Many major lenders, such as large banks, have in-house underwriters. They employ staffs of underwriters who work full-time making sure the lender's money is safe. Smaller lenders may not have the resources to hire full-time underwriters, and they outsource the work to underwriters on a contract basis.

From a borrower's perspective, it doesn't matter which one your lender uses. Any underwriter will review your application with diligence and make sure what you have told them is true and complete.

85. Does every bank employ credit analysts? What do they do?

Almost every lender will have a full-time credit analyst. Banks are in business to make money, and a large part of that comes from interest on loans. Banks have to be careful when they select the people who receive loans. If they give away money to everyone who fills out an application, they won't be in business long. Credit analysts spend their time reviewing the financial strengths and weaknesses of potential borrowers. They make sure borrowers can and will repay loans and minimize the risks lenders face. Lenders are more likely to use credit analysts when they are considering commercial loans than personal ones. What you should learn from this is how important it is for you to present yourself in the best light possible to your lenders because you will have to pass a number of gatekeepers.

86. I made a few errors when I was filling out a loan application. Is that considered fraud?

Don't do anything that will cost you a night's sleep. You don't want to be awake at night wondering if the police are going to knock at your door and haul you down to jail. Before you submit any application, make sure you check all the numbers. It's better to take a few minutes to review an application and correct any problems than to have your bank call you and tell you the numbers don't add up.

Banks and the authorities understand a few honest mistakes. But never intentionally give the bank incorrect information. Lying about how much money you make or omitting financial problems you had in the past is a sure way to find yourself sitting across the table from a police officer or trying to warm the cold steel handcuffs that just became your newest fashion accessory.

Don't forget that if you sign a loan application, you are responsible for the contents being true and complete, even if they were filled out by your accountant. If he lists the wrong houses as being paid for on the application, you are the person who will pay the price. Double check the facts and figures before you sign and submit loan applications.

87. What's the best way to become a successful real estate investor? Is there a school or degree program I can attend?

Wouldn't it be nice if you could sit in a classroom for a few weeks, take a few notes, and then graduate with a piece of paper that tells the world you own an empire?

For a graduation gift, the school could make a nice fat deposit into your bank account and you would never have to work again.

There is no easy way out of it. The only way to become a successful investor is to get out and do it. You have to find deals, rip out drywall, and worry about if tenants are going to pay the rent on time. You have to do things the wrong way and then learn how to do them better. That is the only way to learn how to become a savvy investor.

Of course, along the way you should study and learn as much as you can from investors who have gone before you. If I can toot my own horn, I think the Savvy Landlord series of books are a great way to learn about the industry and mistakes other investors have made while they built their empires. There are other books and authors who can teach you. But there is no substitute for getting your hands dirty and learning the game from the ground up.

88. Where should I store my deeds and other important papers?

You should have a safe place to keep deeds, loan agreements, and all the other documents that you encounter as you grow your business. Sometimes it will seem that you don't own buildings or property. It will seem like what is really important and valuable to a real estate investor are stacks and stacks of paper. You need to keep these in a safe and secure place because if anything happens to them you may be up a creek without a paddle.

Deeds and abstracts can cost a small fortune to replace, especially if you own dozens or hundreds of properties. And without a deed and the title work that goes with it, you may not be able to prove that you own the property. If a tenant stops paying the rent and you don't have a signed copy of her lease, you may have a hard time evicting her. If may not be impossible, but not having a copy of the lease will make the project more challenging (and probably more expensive) than it should be.

Hard copies should be kept in a safe on site or at another location you have easy access to twenty-four hours a day, three hundred and sixty five days a year. A safe deposit at a bank may work when you buy your first few properties, but they will become impractical as your business grows.

I keep electronic copies of all my important documents. As soon as a tenant signs a new lease, I scan it into my computer. I can access it whenever I need to, and a printed version is only a mouse click away. Hard drives and fees for off-site backup sites are extremely inexpensive, and there is no reason why you shouldn't have backup copies of the documents that help you make money.

89. Should I report cash rent payments?

Yes. You should report all your income. If you don't, you might as well put a bulls-eye on the back of your shirt and wait for the IRS to put you in its sights. It can be tempting to think no one will know if you put cash rent payments in your pocket instead of your bank account, but no good will come of that. You will lose a lot of sleep if you ever get audited, and no amount of money will be worth that. Plus, if you don't report all of your income, your business will be undervalued the next time you apply for a loan, and you may not qualify for cash when you need it.

I'm all for not paying one penny more in taxes than I have to, and I hire accountants who spend a lot of time studying and understanding tax rules and regulations. Their job is to help me avoid paying taxes. But pocketing cash payments is known as tax evasion, and that can put you behind bars where you will be on a steady diet of bologna sandwiches. Be savvy. Report your income, take as many deductions as the law allows, and pay the lowest amount of taxes that the law requires.

90. Should I rent to friends or relatives?

Only the ones you don't like and that you want out of your life as soon as possible. Doing business with friends or family is a bad idea. It changes the nature of your relationship, and never in a good way. Expectations change when you rent to people you know. It's not unusual for them to expect to be moved to the top of the list if their toilet needs to be repaired or if one of the doors sticks. There may be pressure for you to cut them a break on the rent. And you will feel awkward if they don't pay their rent on time or if they damage the property.

You will have enough headaches as an investor. Don't create them for yourself. Finding good tenants is hard enough. Don't compound the problem by adding the tension that comes from doing business with your pastor or Aunt Shelia. If you don't take my advice, start looking for a new church and begin thinking of excuses why you can't go to Christmas at Grandma's house this year.

91. Can I make money with new construction rent houses and duplexes?

If the numbers crunch, you can make money on old properties, new properties, borrowed properties, or blue properties. The key is to buy at the right price, put in as little money as the unit needs to be safe when you rent it, and to charge a rent that is reasonable for the property and its location.

However, most investors, including me, build their empires by finding existing (some might say older) houses and duplexes. Many of the properties need work, such as replacing old carpet or fixtures, painting walls, and fixing damaged roofs. We don't pay any more money than we have to for the property, and we negotiate to get the best price on all the work. We use our handymen for every job they are qualified to do, and if we need to we call in one of the prequalified contractors we know will do a good job for a price that won't kill our cash flow. You won't find as many good deals with new properties. If you happen to stumble onto a builder who is having a fire sale you might get a great deal on a unit or two, but don't hold your breath. There are plenty of existing properties you can add to your portfolio.

Here is another way to look at it. Why build when someone already put the money up, and you can get a similar property for half the cost?

92. My tenants split and the husband moved out. The wife and kids can't afford the rent on their own. What do I do?

As I read this question, two landlords appear on my shoulders. On my left is the no-nonsense, all that matters is the money landlord. He doesn't care about anything but getting paid. His response is, "My tenants' marital problems have nothing to do with me. Whoever signed the lease is going to pay every penny for the balance of the lease. I don't care what happens to them or their children."

On my right is the pragmatic, pay it forward, let's try to help people out if they and their children are in a bind landlord. He says, "I may not get my rent for this property without going to court. And then, I still have to collect. Maybe I can move the wife and her children to another one of my properties they can afford. I keep her as a tenant and can look for someone else to rent the unit she is currently living in."

Legally, you could hold the people who signed the lease accountable, and from a business standpoint no one could question your decision.

But sometimes situations like this aren't black and white, and maybe you need to find a creative situation that keeps cash flowing into your bank account. Of course, I'm writing this response a week after Christmas so maybe my business judgment has been clouded by too many carols and overflowing stockings.

93. What is the best business model? Should I buy inexpensive properties that rent for a low amount, or should I buy expensive properties that rent for more money each month?

The best business model is the one that makes you the most money. You have to crunch the numbers on each and every deal to find what works for you. Sometimes, that will be an inexpensive property that rents for a low amount. Other times it will be an expensive property that rents for more money.

The key is to maximize your cash flow. Higher rent does not always equate to more money in your bank account. The property taxes on the property will be higher, as will the mortgage, and those factors will impact how much money you make. Understand the details of each deal and make sure every property fits into your portfolio before you buy it. Be balanced, find your niche, and buy properties that fit it.

94. I rented a property to one person, but I did an inspection today and it looks like twenty people are living there. What do I do?

If you invest in enough properties, this will happen to you. You find someone who appears to be a good tenant and rent to him. But before you know it, your property looks like a frat house. The carpet and grass are worn out from all the foot traffic, and the neighbors complain about the parties.

Your lease should contain a clause that restricts the number of people who can live in one property. And you should know who they are. If your leases don't contain this, contact your attorney as soon as you can.

Don't rent another unit without making sure you can enforce the number of tenants who make your properties their home.

If you find yourself in this situation, start by documenting the number of people who live in the house. Take pictures of people coming and going. Do an inspection inside the house and make notes of what you see. Are clothes piled up to the ceiling? Are there ten different kinds of shampoo in the bathroom?

Once you can confirm that multiple people are living in your property, send the tenant a certified letter and a copy of the lease. Highlight the portion of the lease that restricts how many people can live in the property. If he doesn't take care of the problem, evict him as soon as you can. The more people you live in one of your investments, the quicker it will need to be painted and the quicker the carpet will wear out. Don't let your tenant destroy your portfolio by inviting his friends to live in his crib.

95. Can I perform visual inspections without giving tenants written notice?

Performing visual inspections is a vital part of building your empire. You need to make sure tenants treat your property with care. If you don't inspect your property, you may wind up with a pile of ashes that isn't worth a dime. In many states, you may have to give twenty-hours written notice to inspect a property. There might even be restrictions on the "goodwill" visits you are allowed to make.

Inspecting properties when tenants are not home has downsides, and you can't abuse the privilege. If you keep making repeated unannounced visits to the same apartment you may find yourself on the wrong end of a sexual harassment or racial discrimination suit. And you need to protect yourself. If you feel the need to inspect a property without giving the tenant notice, you may suspect you made a mistake by renting to her. If she is the kind of person you shouldn't have done business with, she may see you as a payday. She may allege you stole a priceless heirloom or the pile of cash she kept under her mattress. If you have to make an unannounced inspection of a property, protect yourself. Take pictures of anything you find or any damage to the property. If you can, take video. You may want to take a witness with you when you inspect properties. I'm not trying to scare you, but don't underestimate what some people are willing to do to make a quick buck.

I give notice by posting a letter on the door and by sending a text message. I don't want any dispute as to whether or not I told a tenant I would inspect her property.

96. When my tenant moved out, he left a bunch of stuff behind. I looked through it and didn't find anything that I wanted to keep. Can I toss it into the trash?

What were you hoping to find? A pile of gold chains that would make most rappers jealous? Wads of cash that would pay for your kids' college tuition?

Property that tenants leave behind should be treated like hand grenades. You don't want to be anywhere near them when they go off. Never look through it hoping to find something you want to keep. In some places, what you can do with property tenants leave behind depends on why they left. If they were evicted, one set of rules applies. If they left voluntarily before the lease expired, another set of rules applies.

Visit with your attorney and find out what your rights and responsibilities are. You don't want to be left holding the bag when your tenant accuses you of stealing his property. At the least, you might get sued. At the worst, you might be charged with theft. Knowing what you can and cannot do will save you headaches and sleepless nights.

Get confirmation by e-mail, text, or voice mail that the tenant has vacated the property. And when you enter the house, take as many pictures as you need to protect yourself.

97. A pipe leaked in one of my properties. The tenant didn't report it, and the water damaged the floors and walls. Can I make the tenant pay for the damage? You are not going to make it easy on me, are you?

You might have a tough time making the tenant pay. I'm no legal expert, and you should take that into account when you read my answer. If it were an issue of normal wear and tear (such as carpet in high-traffic areas that gets worn down), it would probably be up to you to pay for the repairs.

But the situation you describe is more of an issue of negligence, and you may have to prove several things before the tenant would be on the hook to pay for repairs. The first issue would probably be knowledge. Did the tenant actually know about the broken pipe and the water that was coming from it? How big was the leak? Was water spewing from the floor to the ceiling or was it a small leak under the sink or behind the shower that no one could have seen? Was the tenant home when the leak occurred?

Even if the tenant admits he knew about the leak, you may still have another element to prove. Did the tenant act in a reasonable manner once he discovered the leak? Did he call you or a plumber once he found out water was leaking? Did he try to turn off the supply line that feeds water into the house? Did he try to clean up the leak? If he did everything a reasonable person would have done under similar circumstances, you may have a challenge convincing a judge to hold the tenant responsible.

98. What do I need to know about zoning?

As much as you can. Zoning regulations designate how property can be developed and what type of activity it can be used for. Some areas are designated as residential areas. Other areas are designated for use as commercial, retail, or industrial sites. If you invest in commercial properties, you need to make sure prospective properties are properly zoned for how your tenants want to use them. If your tenant wants to operate a strip mall, he doesn't want or need to look at residential or industrial properties. If you build a new building or structure, verify that it will be properly zoned when it is finished. You don't want to invest your time or money on a project that you will never be able to finish.

You have the right to petition the zoning boards to have property re-zoned. But its additional time and expense, and the uncertainty may not be worth the effort.

If you invest in residential property, you need to look at the how the property around yours is zoned. The property that is near yours can have a substantial impact on the value of your investments. If the vacant lot on the backside of two of your houses suddenly becomes an industrial park or is developed into a warehouse, you may lose thousands of dollars. And the property may become less attractive to many potential tenants.

Knowledge is power. Know how the property near yours is zoned, and keep track of what is happening with the local planning commission. Any plans for development that might impact your portfolio will be a matter of public record, and you won't be shocked when bulldozers show up and start to build a shopping mall. Check the local paper or business journal to monitor any new developments or changes to zoning regulations.

99. My tenant wants to run a business out of the home. Is this okay?

Generally speaking, I am in favor of anything that helps my tenants pay the rent on time. If he wants to open a business and sign the checks over to me, that wouldn't be a problem. But I don't want my properties to be used as someone else's warehouse or manufacturing plant.

Many people work out of their homes. They answer e-mails, telecommute, and write proposals in their pajamas. I would need to know more about the business before I could make a decision. If he was a writer or day trader I wouldn't say anything. But if he wants to sell clothing out of the garage and the street traffic goes through the roof we would have a problem. The same would be true if he needed to install a commercial furnace so that he could melt iron and cast engine blocks. As long as his business didn't damage the value of the property or interfere with my neighbors' ability to use theirs, I wouldn't make an issue out of it.

100. What accommodations do I need to make for handicapped tenants? Do I have to install ramps or modify bathrooms?

This is not an easy question to answer. The rules and regulations are covered by state and federal law, and you need to consult your attorney to make sure you are handling issues properly when dealing with handicapped tenants. But here are some general rules. You cannot refuse to rent to someone because he is disabled. If you discriminate against people because they need a walker or wheelchair, you are an idiot and will get what you deserve. If a tenant asks for a reasonable accommodation, you have to comply and allow it to happen. For example, if a tenant needs handrails installed in the bathroom, you have to grant access for a handyman to enter the property. You don't have to pay for the modifications, and you can pass the costs along to the tenant.

You should also consider having your handyman doing the work. You know he will do good work at a decent price, and you know where to find him if things don't go as planned. It's a good method of ensuring quality work on your properties.

It can be tempting to look at modifications as a burden or another expense you shouldn't have to incur. But there is a more positive way to look at things. By installing modifications, you are increasing the number of tenants who are able to rent your investments, and that means money in your pocket. It's a win-win. Disabled tenants have more quality places to live, and you have a larger pool of potential renters.

101. What's the best way to keep up with changes in real estate laws that impact me?

When you ask this question, it makes me feel warm. You are becoming wise, and you want to stop problems before they start. There are many things you should do to stay on top of changes in real estate laws. You should hire an attorney who specializes in real estate and has experience with investors. She should belong to local and national associations that monitor changes in real estate and landlord-tenant law. When something changes, hopefully she will let you know and tell you how to adjust. Your local REIA club is another great way to learn about new laws or changes to old ones. Some clubs may even have speakers who talk about important issues or changes at the end of the year. Don't be afraid to find a veteran investor and ask him as many questions as you can. You also need to educate yourself. Read as much as you can, and research local and federal laws that affect how you run your business. There are several good websites devoted to educating real estate investors. Monitor them frequently, and don't hesitate to send an e-mail if something isn't clear.

Knowledge is power. The more of it you have, the better off you will be.

102. I'm moving out of state. Should I hire a property manager to care for my properties, or sell out and buy rentals in my new hometown?

Step over here and let me slap you. One of the best advantages to owning rental properties is that you don't have to be near it to manage it. Before you buy your first property, one of your goals should be to build a company that runs on autopilot. You should hire a property manager as soon as you own enough properties to justify it. She will make sure your tenants pay on time and that all repairs get done. You can sit back on a beach somewhere or on your couch for the rest of your life.

It will take years for you to get to the point where you can justify hiring a property manager. If you sell out and start over in a new place, you will be reinventing the wheel. Don't throw away all of your hard work. Be savvy. Turn the work over to someone else and enjoy yourself. Of course, once you get to your new location and understand the market, feel free to invest there if it makes sense.

103. What is the best way to pass on my real estate to my kids? Do I have to worry about estate taxes?

The best way to transfer property to your children will depend on your situation. There isn't one simple answer. But here is the worst way: do nothing. If you don't talk to your attorney about how to make sure your family is taken care of, you might as well kiss your empire goodbye. Passing wealth to your children can be tricky, and there are a number of options you might consider. These include trusts, corporations, and family corporations. Your team of professionals will tell you what the right fit is for you and your situation.

Remember to be flexible. You circumstances may change. You may get divorced (although I hope you don't), or your empire may grow so large you need to look at other options to make sure your property goes where you want it to. What works for you today may not work in ten years. Keep that in mind, and review your estate planning with your attorney on a recurring basis. And familiarize yourself with the details surrounding 1031 exchanges.

104. Should my rehab crew and handyman be employees of my company?

There are advantages both ways. If they are employees, you have to consider paying worker's comp, withholding taxes, and making sure you have enough work to keep them busy. You don't want to pay people to sit around all day. You also have to consider liability issues. If an employee has a wreck while driving to a job site, your company may be held liable. If your handyman and rehab crew are independent contractors, they are responsible for their taxes, and you don't have to pay workers' compensation. They are responsible for finding work. If there are no jobs available, you aren't subsidizing them sitting around and drinking coffee.

The big disadvantage of treating them as independent contractors is that they may not be available when you need them. If they are good at what they do, other investors will want to use them. One of your properties may need to be painted before it is ready to be rented. You want it done as quickly as possible, because every day that passes means money out of your pocket. But your handyman can't get to it until next week because he is replacing carpet for another investor. If he and his crew were employees, you could dictate which job he worked on, but as an independent contractor he gets to make the call.

When your company is large enough to justify the expense, you should consider hiring a full-time handyman and crew. You will have enough work to keep them busy, and the numbers will add up. In the meantime, find a handyman and crew you like and give them as much work as you can. Pay them on time, and do what you can to keep them happy. Hopefully, when they have the choice between working for you or another investor, they will choose you.

For the record, I prefer to keep them as independent contractors. It makes my life simpler.

105. **I enjoy managing my properties. Should I go into the management business?**

Easy, Sparky. Don't jump the gun. Enjoying taking care of your property doesn't mean you will enjoy, or be good at, managing properties other investors own. When you are managing your own investments, you have a sense of ownership. Every call you make to a handyman is an investment in your family's future. You want the work to be done well so that your portfolio grows. It matters to you in a way that managing property for others won't.

Managing property for others can quickly feel like a job. You are working for someone else. Instead of building your portfolio, you are building someone else's. You don't receive the benefit that working on your investments gives you.

But the biggest reason you shouldn't consider managing anyone else's property is that you shouldn't be managing anyone's investments, including your own. The goal is to build a company that runs itself. It doesn't need you to manage it because you have hired other people to do that. Of course, if you like managing properties as a hobby, then have at it. And if you enjoy it that much, give me a call. You sound like a person I should have on my team.

106. What am I allowed to say about a bad tenant when another landlord calls for a reference?

You are not asking the right question. The right question is, "What should I say when another landlord calls for a reference about a bad tenant?

" You can tell the truth. You can say that the tenant didn't pay his rent on time, that when he left the property it looked like crap and you didn't refund any of his security deposit. You can say that the tenant scared the rest of the neighborhood and you got several calls about him.

But is that the best thing to do? Is that the best way to invest your time?

Consider having a stock response for inquiries about bad tenants. Something generic, such as, "The only thing I will say about Mr. Jones is that he is no longer a tenant." Any savvy landlord will understand what that means. They will recognize you have a lot to say but are choosing not to. And if the landlord is not savvy and he rents to the tenant anyway, he will hear your words loud and clear when he is wasting a day sitting in small claims court.

It can be tempting to consider saying something petty when you are called about bad tenants. It's human nature to want to tell the world about how he left you high and dry. Don't be petty. Saying bad things about people, even when they are true, can put you in a bad spot. If the tenant finds out what you said and doesn't like it, he may get mad enough to sue you for defamation. Then you will have to pay to have the suit tossed out, even if it is worthless.

Take the high road. That is where empires are built and where dreams come true. Grinding an axe against some loser who skipped out on his rent isn't good for you or your family, and it won't help you pay the bills next month.

107. Should I pay myself a salary for managing or rehabbing my properties?

I hope you aren't doing it for free. The whole point of the enterprise is to turn your blood, sweat, and dreams into a big pile of cash. Whether or not you should pay yourself a salary for managing or rehabbing depends on your situation, and you should consult your tax professional before cutting the check.

When I managed and rehabbed my properties without any outside help, I never directly paid myself. I kept my money and invested it in the business, and that helped my company grow. But I was rewarded in other ways. My work increased the value of the property and increased my knowledge of how the investing business works. It taught me the business from the ground up, and I wouldn't have the monster business I have today if I didn't pay my dues in the early days.

108. Can I use a personal check when I close on a property?

You can, but you need to use whatever form of payment helps your company grow the fastest. You also want to create as big a paper trail as is possible so that when tax season rolls around you can document all your personal and company expenses. Make it easy for your accountant to save you money.

I wouldn't use a personal check at a closing. The title company doesn't care as long as the check will clear. But my company is set up as a corporation, and I want to make sure all of my corporate expenses come out of my corporate account. I don't want to miss out on any deductions or give anyone the ability to pierce the corporate veil. Plus, many title companies prefer cashier's checks, and using a personal check might delay closing.

Always operate your company using the highest and best business practices. Pay attention to detail, even on the smallest thing such as choosing which account you use when you write a check. That creates the best foundation and ensures your business will last. Using a personal check for a business transaction may not be the best way of doing business and should be avoided when possible.

109. Should I partner with an investor?

Yes, when it helps you build your portfolio and grow your company. Partnering with other investors on certain projects can help you leverage their cash, experience, and connections. It can shorten the time it takes for your empire to grow and get you to the finish line more quickly than you could on your own.

But you have to be careful to choose the right investor to do business with. Don't partner with someone because he is a nice guy or your kids carpool to school together. Partners should have a track record of doing profitable deals, and your skill sets should compliment each other. You don't want to be tethered to the wrong person.

And it needs to be the right project. If you are trying to buy an apartment complex, but neither one of you has ever operated a multi-dwelling unit, you may need to pass on the deal. If both of you have experience in residential properties but none in commercial, you may not want to start looking at strip malls for sale.

110. **What is a title insurance policy exception?**

Title insurance is one of the best investments you will make as you build your portfolio. Owning real estate is different than owning almost anything else, especially in the fact that when you own real estate you have to prove clear title. You have to hire someone to perform an abstract, which is a document that traces the history of ownership of the property and proves no one else can make a claim of ownership.

Once the title work has been done and approved, the insurance company has a duty to protect the homeowner from anyone who tries to claim ownership of the property. But there are certain exceptions to policies where the title company won't have to defend your claim of ownership. A few of the more common exemptions include easements and rights of way, zoning and building restrictions, and certain undisclosed factors, including mechanic's liens and certain taxes and special assessments.

The takeaway is to understand that you should buy title insurance on every property, but there are a few situations where the insurance company may not have to pay. With this information, you know to ask the title company about any exceptions that may apply. You also know to look under a few more rocks and see a few more potholes you should avoid.

111. **I heard an investor talk about forced appreciation. What is that?**

I wish it meant that all of your friends and family made you go to dinner, where they all told you how much they loved you, whether you wanted to hear it or not. Unfortunately, it is not nearly as romantic. Forced appreciation is another term for the profit you make when you buy property low and sell it high. It's the transactional profit of selling property. It is also known as traditional appreciation, because it is what most people think of when they hear the word "appreciation."

Some people contrast it with automatic appreciation, which is used to describe the increase in value of a property that occurs naturally when you buy the right property in the right location at the right time. If you do your due diligence, you know areas in your market that are hot. Families want to move into certain school districts, and certain parts of town become more desirable. Neighborhoods have a cycle of desirability, and if you buy at the right time the value of your portfolio can increase exponentially overnight.

112. Someone told me I was "unbankable." What does that mean?

It's a huge insult, and if it's true it may mean the end of your investing career. It means you are too big of a credit risk to get a loan from a traditional lender. It's another way of saying you are a deadbeat, and no one wants to do business with you. As an investor, you have to have access to other people's cash. If you can't borrow you can't grow. And if you don't grow, you are dead in the water. You will never have enough cash to buy all of your properties without taking out loans. If you did, you wouldn't need to learn how to invest. And you would lose many of the best deductions that are allowed under the tax code when you borrow money, such as the deduction for interest.

If traditional lenders consider you unbankable, you will need to look elsewhere to find cash. There are plenty of nontraditional, private lenders, but they come with a cost. It's usually in the form of higher interest rates and fees, and if you use nontraditional lenders you need to crunch the numbers and make sure the higher monthly payments you will pay work for you.

113. What's the difference between asset management and property management?

They sound similar, but are worlds apart. And you need to use both of them. Asset management refers the team of people who help you manage your money, such as investing it in the stock market or bonds.

When you make a big stack of cash, you need to put it somewhere, and you can't put it all in real estate. Diversification is important. You don't want to put all of your eggs in one basket, and your asset management team will help reduce your risk and maximize your security.

Property management refers to the people who oversee the day-to-day operations of being a landlord. They collect the rent, pay the property taxes, and arrange for any needed repairs. They make it possible for you to enjoy owning property without having to deal with the headaches associated with it. If you pick the right property management team, you will sleep well and wake up every day to the smell of money.

114. **What is a pocket listing?**

If you know the right realtors, pocket listings can be a goldmine. Pocket listings are exclusive rights to sell, where the seller of a property gives a real estate agent the sole right to find a buyer of a property. The property is never advertised as being for sale. The agent contacts people who might be interested in buying the property, and if things fall into place, the property can be sold quickly. Get to know as many real estate agents in your area as you can. You never know when one of them will call with a sweet deal that would fit into your portfolio.

115. **My realtor asks for my highest and best offer whenever I submit a proposal. How should I handle this?**

This is one of my pet peeves. It makes me feel like realtors are trying to get me to negotiate against myself. They want me to tell them the maximum amount of money I am willing to pay for a property, and I wonder if I could get it for a cheaper amount.

There is a pattern to negotiating, and I don't like being forced to automatically jump to the highest amount I am willing to pay. Especially when the person doing the pushing is earning a commission.

I've tried to avoid this by limiting the number of agents I work with. I won't deal with any that push me to submit my highest offer right off the bat. If you have a better solution, I would love to hear it.

116. What's the difference between a line of credit and lending limit?

It's the difference between cash in the bank and a dream about money. A line of credit is an available amount of funds that your bank has approved. It works like a credit card. It has a set limit, and when you pay down the balance you can borrow against it again. It is usually secured by your property.

A lending limit is a term bankers use for funds that have been set aside in case a borrower has a need in the future. It's similar to being preapproved for a loan, but the borrower never signs anything, and the bank can withdraw the line at any time. I have also been told that some bankers use the terms interchangeably. If you have any doubts or confusion about how your banker is using them, be sure to ask.

117. Does a proof of funds letter really mean anything?

A proof of funds letter is a document from a lender telling a seller that the buyer has funds available to purchase a property. They are often used in cash deals, and they are used to prequalify buyers. The right proof of funds letters can make your life much easier. The wrong ones aren't worth the paper they are written on.

The key is to make sure they are legitimate. Anyone can bring in a piece of paper stating they have money in the bank. But I wouldn't bet my kids' college funds on that. Before I had any confidence in a proof of funds letter, I would contact the bank and talk to the person who signed it. Once confirmed, and I have confidence that the letter is legitimate, I would assume that the person offering it is serious and has the funds available to make the deal happen.

118. **What does DOM mean?**

DOM stands for "days on market." It refers to the number of days a property has been listed with a realtor on the MLS. The higher the DOM the more motivated the seller may be. It's important to know the DOM because a seller may not be willing to negotiate the price of a property if it has only been on the market for five days. But if it has been on the market for 105 days, you have a much better shot of making a deal at 20 percent below the asking price. Realtors will be able to tell you the DOM of a property, but you can also go to Zillow.com and educate yourself.

119. **What is discounted paper?**

Discounted paper is a promissory note being sold for less than what the note is worth, and can be a savvy way to build your portfolio. Paper, or loans, have a face value. Assume the face value of a 10 percent loan is $20,000, and full payment, including interest is due in one year (a total of $22,000). The person holding the note may need cash and offer to sell the note at a discounted rate, such as $18,000. The purchaser of this loan would be paid $22,000 and make $4,000 or 22.22%. Not a bad deal. Keep your ears to the ground and try to find people willing to sell paper at discounted rates.

120. **I've heard several other investors talk about a credibility kit. What is that?**

Part of your job as an investor is to meet people. You have to make cold calls and approach people who own property you want to buy or who can help you finance deals. When you are a new investor meeting private investors for the first time, you have to establish as much credibility as quickly as you can. A credibility kit is a resume on steroids. It is a polished biography that includes your experience as an investor, a description or list of the deals you have done, and any classes or seminar you have attended. As your career advances, you may have the opportunity to speak at seminars or publish articles about investing. Those should be included in your credibility kit.

The idea is to separate yourself from all the other investors who are also looking for properties and trying to get deals done. A well-written and professional looking credibility kit will help you get your foot in the door and will create opportunities. Create one as soon as you can and carry copies of it in your truck.

121. **What is lis pendens?**

If you own real estate, you never want to hear this Latin phrase. It means that someone has filed a formal notice asserting a claim against your property. They are saying they own it and want a judge to issue an order taking it from you.

That expression is one of the reasons you need title insurance on every property. If someone files a lis pendens action against you and you have title insurance, the insurance company has to pay for your defense against the claim. They have to hire the lawyers who fight on your behalf. Title insurance is a few hundred dollars. Defending yourself in a lis pendens action will cost thousands. It's an easy choice, isn't it?

122. **What is private trustee sale?**

A private trustee is the person who has been appointed to control a trust established by an individual or family. If you haven't talked to your attorney about using a trust as part of your estate planning or as a way to own property, make sure to add that to your to-do list. A private trustee sale happens when a trustee sells property that is owned by the trust. The funds go into the trust and are held for the benefit of the beneficiaries.

A public trustee is an individual appointed by a court (usually a bankruptcy court) and oversees property owned by a company or person who has filed for bankruptcy. When the property is sold, the funds are divided and distributed to creditors of the estate.

123. I heard some investors talking about the Fed. What is that? Does that mean I have to worry about my houses being raided by the FBI?

It sounds scary, but when people talk about the Fed, they are referring to the Federal Reserve System. The Fed is the central banking system for the United States, and it sets many of the economic policies for banks throughout the country.

As an investor, the primary reason you need to know about the Fed is that it determines the prime interest rate, which is the rate banks pay when they borrow money. When the Fed raises its rate, banks raise theirs and pass the cost on to you. The Fed also regulates banks and other lenders, and its policies may make it difficult for you to borrow money.

124. What are short sales?

Short sales are gold mines for investors, and you should try to find as many of them as you can afford and that fit in your portfolio. A short sale happens when a property owner is facing foreclosure and he owes more on the house than what it is worth. The bank holding the note is willing to sell the house for less than what is owed on it. The amount paid is short of the amount owed, and the bank can try to go after the original owner to collect the difference. As an investor, short sales can help you find properties at discounted prices from motivated sellers. Keep your ear to the ground, scour your area for signs advertising auctions, and hopefully you can buy properties as a short sale that increase your cash flow.

125. A plumber repaired pipes in one of my properties three months ago. He hasn't sent me a bill yet. What should I do?

Shame on the plumber for not having better billing practices. Learn from his mistake, and make sure that your invoices go out on time and that everyone pays you as promised.

You need to track down the plumber and make sure you can document paying him for services rendered. It's the right thing to do, but it may also save you legal trouble down the road. Contractors who work on your property have the right to file mechanic or materialmen liens on property if they haven't been paid. That will cloud your title and make it difficult or impossible for you to sell a property.

If you don't make sure the plumber is paid, he may catch his billing problem at the end of the year and blame you for the problem. The next morning he may wander down to the courthouse and file a lien. It will cost you more than the plumbing bill to resolve the problem.

126. **What is an internal rate of return (IRR)?**

Investors use many different ways to determine if a deal will make enough money and to compare deals to see which one is worth sinking money into. Some investors like to use IRR because it looks at rates of return rather than the present value of property. IRR looks at the expected return on an investment over time, and the higher the IRR the better the deal. I won't bore you by trying to explain how to do it here, but software like Excel and most financial calculators will help you determine an investment's IRR.

127. **What is a lease option?**

A lease option is a lease agreement where the renter has the right to purchase the property sometime in the future. The price is usually set at the time the contract is signed, and the renter pays a down payment.

Lease options are great options for buyers who can't secure traditional financing, and they are great for investors because properties under lease options usually sell for higher prices.

The gist is that lease options are awesome for investors. You keep the cash flow, because the renter is paying you every month until the purchase price is paid in full. But you don't have to do any of the maintenance. The purchaser is required to perform any needed repairs, and you won't have to answer calls in the middle of the night about leaky faucets. You get all the benefit of owning the property with none of the burdens.

128. **What is a sandwich lease?**

Sandwiches. Yum.

A sandwich lease (also known as a lease option with a sandwich lease) happens when a renter rents the property to someone else. It's also known as subletting. It is not unusual, and happens frequently in commercial real estate when a tenant can no longer afford the rent on a property.

129. **What is a double-closing?**

Double closings are some of the best deals you will ever make. In a traditional closing, there is one buyer and one seller. The parties transfer title to a property and the deal is done. In a double-closing, there are three parties. Party 1 sells the property to Party 2, who then sells it to Party 3. Party 2 is both a buyer and a seller.

Double-closings can be a great way to make quick cash, especially if you are Party 2. You buy undervalued property from Party 1 and sell it at a quick profit to Party 3. Everybody wins, and the man in the middle makes a bunch of cash.

130. **What is an assignable contract?**

An assignable contract allows one or both parties to transfer their rights under the contract to another party. That party then has the same rights and responsibilities as the original party. As an investor, someone may make you a sweet deal on a property and you want to cash out instead of banking on the cash flow the property generates, and that's where assignability contracts can help. Generally speaking, however, contracts have to have clauses that permit assignability. Check with your attorney to make sure your agreement can be assigned before discussing the possibility.

131. **What are flood zones and how do they work? Can they change? Why do I need a flood certificate?**

A flood zone is a way to measure the risk of your property being flooded. It is a way to assess the risk of insuring a property, and depending where your property is you may have to pay higher insurance rates or not be eligible for insurance at all. The zones are established by FEMA, and you can access their maps online.

The zones are determined by looking at historical data (how often has the property flooded in the past) and location. Properties near rivers or the ocean may be determined to be a higher risk.

You need a certificate for every property that is secured by a mortgage. Your lenders will want to know every risk associated with your properties, and flooding is one of those. If you are new to investing and your lender asks about a flood certificate don't stress. It happens on every loan, and you will get used to it as you do more deals.

132. **What is a spec sheet?**

A spec sheet is a simple document that lists all the specifications for a property. It has the square footage, the year the house was built, how many bedrooms and bathrooms, and many other details about your properties. Sellers will use them as a short biography of the property. It's a great way to get relevant information to buyers and help them decide if the property is one they should buy.

133. **What is an estoppel letter?**

Estoppel is a legal principle that may prevent a party from denying facts based on their conduct. It has several uses in real estate. If you buy an apartment building, you want the seller to sign an estoppel letter saying the tenants are current on the rent. You don't want to purchase a great building only to realize no one has paid rent in three months.

Also, some of the properties you buy will be in areas that are governed by homeowners associations. HOAs have broad powers, including being able to put liens on property if the owners do not pay HOA dues. An estoppel from an HOA documents what the seller does or doesn't owe the HOA. If the seller owes association dues, it's important to resolve that issue before closing. If not, the buyer may not have clear title to the property or the closing may be delayed. That means additional time and expense, and those are two words you don't want to hear as an investor.

134. **Can you explain deferred maintenance?**

Yes. Deferred maintenance is not a good thing. It is a term appraisers use to describe property that has not been maintained as it should have been. Maybe the roof needs to be replaced or the exterior needs to be painted.

If you are buying a property, deferred maintenance can help you negotiate a better deal. You can drop your offer because you will have to invest more money in the property to get it ready to rent. As a seller or owner, deferred maintenance means you need to spend money on the property or face selling it at a bargain price. The savvy way to run your business it to maintain all of your properties like you were living in them. Don't wait for the roof to fly off during a storm or for wood to rot. Do regular maintenance and the value of your properties will grow.

135. **Is there a grading system for properties?**

Multi-family units are graded by a system that ranks them from A to D. Just like it was when you were in third grade English, A is the best and D is the worst. The most important factor is age. Properties that are brand new or up to fifteen years old are A grade, while B properties are fifteen to thirty years old. C grade properties were built thirty to forty-five years ago, while D properties are at least forty-five years old. Condition, amenities, and location also make a difference. A properties are in the best locations and have all the newest features, while D grade units are old, featureless properties in the least desirable part of the market.

But the most important grading system is, "How much money will this investment put in my pockets?" That's the simple answer. But there are a lot of ways to look at that. For some investors, that means how much profit they will make when they flip it. For others, it is how much cash flow they will generate over the life of the property.

We have already looked at some ways to grade investments, including IRR. You have to find a method that works for you and that you understand. Some deals will come down to a gut feeling. It either feels like a deal that works for you or you know you should stay clear of it. You can't put your finger on it or make a chart out of it. You just know it's not going to work.

136. I filed an insurance claim on one of my roofs, but didn't use the proceeds to have it replaced. The roof looks good and doesn't leak. Is it okay to keep the money?

Here are a few things to think about. Your bank has an interest in the property. That's the purpose of a mortgage lien. It makes sure the bank is protected throughout the life of the loan. If the roof was a complete loss, it diminishes the value of your home. If you don't replace the roof, your banker will not be happy. And you want to keep your banker happy.

The bigger issue may be insurance related. When you decide to sell the property, the home may not be insurable until a new roof is installed. And that means new buyers may not be willing or able to complete the deal. That will slow down or prevent a deal from closing, and that will impact your bottom line.

You will eventually have to replace the roof. Make sure that doesn't happen at a time when paying a roofer ruins your cash flow. Not having the roof repaired is a gamble, and you should think twice about risking parts of your empire.

137. I just completed repairs on one of my properties. Should I have another appraisal done?

No. You should only have appraisals done when a lender requires it before issuing a loan, or when you begin investing and don't feel comfortable judging the value of a property. If you do it more often than that, you are wasting money.

138. What is a non-recourse loan, and how do I get one?

In every landlord's dream world, it rains $100 bills and all the loans are non-recourse. Non-recourse loans are secured by property, but the borrower has no individual liability. Suppose you own a property and a lender has secured a loan by placing a lien on the property. Under a traditional loan, if you default the bank can sue you or your company if the proceeds from the sale of the property don't cover the amount owed. If you have a non-recourse loan, once the property is sold the lender has to take the loss and can't sue you or your company. If you know lenders that approve non-recourse loans, please let me know. I would love to put them on speed dial.

139. What type of insurance policy do you purchase for your rental properties? Do you buy replacement cost or actual cash value?

You need to understand the difference between these types of policies. Replacement value policies pay you the cost of items or repairs at today's value. If you have to put a new roof on a property and it costs $5,000, you get paid $5,000. Under actual cash value, you would be paid replacement value minus depreciation. Depending on the age of the item, that can be substantial.

I buy replacement cost policies. The monthly premiums are more, but the extra protection gives me peace of mind.

140. I maxed out my bank. How can I borrow more money so that I can buy more properties?

To build a great portfolio, you have to use more than one bank. I used my bank to acquire ten properties and maxed out the $500,000 lending limit. I refinanced the properties at another bank, and that freed up my lending limit at the first bank. I borrowed from them and repeated.

The key is to buy houses at 65 to 70 percent of the market value so there is room to refinance with the second bank. It's a quick way to build your empire.

141. I am preparing to meet with a bank to apply for my first loan. How should I act?

Be as professional as possible. You don't have to put on an act and try to be someone you aren't, but there are a few simple things you can do to increase the odds you will be approved. Be on time. It's rude to be late. Dress professionally. You don't have to buy an expensive suit, but don't wear the coveralls you used last week when you crawled under one of your properties trying to find a sewer leak.

And the most important thing to do is to have your financial documents in order. Make sure you have your income and expense reports prepared and documented in a clear and simple way. Don't give your banker any reason to turn you down.

142. What is a due-on-sale clause?

Most mortgages have provisions that require the borrower to pay off the balance of the loan immediately if the property is sold or if the title changes hands. The idea is that banks have the right to know the people they are lending money to. When you fill out a loan application, the bank goes through your credit history and finances with a fine-tooth comb. They only give you a check after they feel confident you are a good credit risk and will pay off the loan as you agreed. If you sell the property and the balance is transferred to the purchaser, the bank would have no way to evaluate its risk. It might have to write off a load of bad debt it never agreed to. As an investor, keep in mind that if you flip or sell properties you will probably have to cut the bank a check after the closing. If you assume you can keep all of the funds and then have to cough up a big pile of cash to the bank, it may cost you your empire. And you may find your name and picture on the front page of the local paper, but not in a good way.

These clauses became popular after the 1980s, when people were assuming loans left and right. Banks needed to protect themselves from their loans being transferred to people who couldn't pay them, and the clauses have become standard contract language.

143. **I did my first five deals and love being an investor. I'm ready to turn my business into an empire. How can I find more properties?**

Awesome. That's the kind of talk I like to hear. I love it when people get off the couch and make things happen.

Two ways to find great deals most people take for granted are direct mailing campaigns and signs. You should find a way to include both as part of your marketing. Direct mailing can be an effective and inexpensive way to build your portfolio. Direct marketing can work one of two ways. You should have an idea of where you want to own properties. Search areas where you understand the value of the properties, the nature of the neighborhoods, and that have a high potential for growth because of their desirability or location. One approach is to send out letters to the owner of every property in the area outlining your desire to buy their property. Flood the entire area with letters and hope that the right people will respond. If there are hundreds of houses in the area, it can seem like a daunting and expensive task. You don't have to send all the letters out at once. Break it up into smaller parts and it will be more manageable and affordable.

Don't forget to network with local wholesalers. They will do all the work for you. They will find properties, get them under contract, and offer you a deal where you can both make money. All you have to do is look at the property and see if it fits your portfolio.

144. **What time of the month should I close a deal?**

You should close a deal any time you find a property that makes you money and fits into your portfolio. It doesn't matter if it is the first day of the month, the last, or any day in between. All that matters is that the numbers add up.

But there are a few things to keep in mind. If you close in the middle of the month, there may be an issue involving prorated rent. The seller may be entitled to a portion of the rents because he owned the property for half the month. And you may want to push the first mortgage payment six weeks from the closing date. This would allow you to collect rents and use them to make the first mortgage payment. You wouldn't have any more money out of pocket, and that should make you smile. Unless sitting on a big stack of cash makes you cry.

In my experience, however, there are certain seasons where deals are more likely to get done. No one seems to do much business in the winter. Maybe it's too cold for them. Maybe they have made enough money for that calendar year. Whatever the reason, it seems like there is a lag at the end of the year when only a few deals get done. And that might be an opportunity for an aggressive investor like you to make things happen. If you are out in the cold working like a madman when your competitors are staying warm and cozy in their houses, you will beat them to the finish line.

145. **What is an enrolled agent?**

When you build your team of professionals, one of the people you should consider hiring is an enrolled agent. Enrolled agents are similar to accountants and are authorized to represent people when they are facing an audit or collection issues with the IRS. Many of them are former IRS agents, and they undergo extensive testing to become an EA.

While your CPA can be an EA, they differ from CPAs in that EAs focus on tax returns and resolving disputes. CPAs are more specialized and tend to focus on business planning, accounting services, and preparing taxes.

Hiring an EA can give you a huge advantage, in that they offer the best of both worlds. They can help you plan your business so that you take advantage of all the deductions you are entitled to and represent you in court if you ever face an audit.

146. **What should I get at closing?**

I love closings. They are like the first day of spring, when I see $100 bills blossoming on money trees. I have always thought that title companies should include cookies and milk at closings. That would make them almost perfect.

If you are the seller, you should get a fat check. It represents your hard work and the wisdom you displayed when you bought the property.

If you are a buyer, you should receive a new property that fits into your portfolio because you crunched the numbers and did your due diligence. You should also receive the keys. And make sure you have visited with your insurance agent and that the property is covered. Then you can get the property ready to rent and make some money.

If the property has tenants, you should also receive a complete rent roll with the tenants' Social Security numbers, complete and current leases, and their payment histories.

147. **How do real estate auctions work?**

Real estate auctions are simple to understand. Property is offered for sale, and whoever bids the most money buys the property. You can scour your local newspaper to find auctions near you, and you can also find online auctions. Auctions can be a great way to build your portfolio.

A few things to keep in mind. Make sure you have cash to buy the property or have financing arranged before the auction begins. You will have to pay for the property fairly quickly after the auction ends, and you may not have time to be approved. And some auctions have a minimum reserve, which means that if it isn't sold for a certain price the deal is off. Those without reserve are final when the gavel hits the podium.

When you buy property from an auction, you generally receive it in fee absolute, which means it won't be subject to any liens or encumbrances. Unless you financed the property and the lender needs to put a lien on it.

One of the easiest purchases I made was through hubzu.com. It was incredibly simple, and I didn't have to leave the office other than to make my initial inspection of the property. You may also consider auction. com. Happy bidding.

148. **What contingencies should I have in my offer?**

Many offers have contingencies, which are conditions that must be met before a closing becomes final. One of the most common contingencies is that the property must pass an inspection. In many deals, the buyer and seller want to make sure the property is ready to be inhabited. An inspector is paid to come out to the property and make sure there are no major problems. Buyers generally don't want to buy a property if they are going to have to invest thousands of dollars in it before it can be rented, and an inspection contingency is a good way to protect themselves in case there are issues with a property. I do a quick inspection before I buy any properties. Some of the houses I buy are bargains because there are issues with them. I'm getting the properties at bargain prices, and know that I will have to spend some money before I can rent them. But I have done enough deals and have enough experience to know what will need to be done and what it will cost. I can crunch the numbers without an inspector's help. And some of my deals are done on such a tight timeline I can't get an inspection done before closing.

Financing contingencies are also common. If the buyer is not able to secure financing, the deal won't close. Another contingency that is becoming common is an insurance contingency. Buyers want to make sure properties can be insured before closing becomes final. No one wants to be stuck paying for a house that can't be insured. That would cause a lot of lost sleep. I can imagine a landlord staying up a lot of nights wondering if tonight was the night an uninsurable house would burn down.

It's important to know what contingencies are in your offers, and what your rights and responsibilities are. And you should always negotiate the costs of any contingencies. If your deal has an inspection contingency, make sure the other party foots the bill. It may only be a few hundred dollars, but when you multiply that by the number of properties in your empire, it adds up.

149. **What is a table closing?**

A table closing is where all the parties to a real estate deal meet face to face to exchange any documents and make sure all the contingencies have been met. One of the benefits is that it puts pressure on everyone to make sure they have everything done before the meeting. People don't want to show up, look everyone else in the eyes, and tell them the closing will have to be rescheduled because they didn't do what they were supposed to do.

Another kind of closing is an escrow closing. The parties never meet, and all the documents are exchanged at different times and places. There is usually a schedule for an escrow closing, but there is not the kind of pressure to get the deal done that comes with table closings.

150. **What are abstracts? Where should I store them?**

An abstract is a written record that details the chain of ownership of a piece of real property. It shows every time the property has changed ownership, and has a certificate from the abstractor that the abstract is complete. You will need an abstract of every piece of property. Paying a mortgage doesn't mean anything if you can't prove you own the property.

You should keep your abstracts in a safe place where you have easy access. You don't want them to get wet in a flood or damaged in a fire. Safe deposit boxes won't be a good option because most of them aren't big enough to hold all the abstracts from your empire, and you won't have access unless the bank is open. There probably won't be a situation where you have to run get an abstract in an emergency, but if you keep your abstracts in a safe, waterproof place on site you will have access whenever you need it. There are storage companies that offer climate-controlled areas, but they come with an additional expense. Make sure you crunch the numbers if you decide to rent one.

Another great option is to store them with the title company. Their goal is to keep you as a customer, and if they hold the abstracts you will need to have contact with them.

151. **Is it true you can become wealthy in your spare time?**

Yes. Becoming wealthy in your spare time is easy. All you have to do is inherit a lot of money or become an expert at picking winning lottery numbers. Another great option is to put a band together over the course of a weekend and sell a million albums before going on a world tour.

Building true wealth is not easy. If it were, everyone would do it. People who sell products claiming that you can make millions of dollars with little or no effort cannot be trusted. Investing in real estate is a great opportunity. It can help you provide a lifestyle for your family that most people only dream of. Anyone can do it, but it takes work. You have to find properties, get financing, rehab properties, and find the right tenants. But it becomes easier the more you do it, and if you do it the right way you can build something special.

152. **When should I hire a CPA? What services should I expect?**

You should hire a CPA before you buy your first property. It may seem like you won't need one if you only have one property, but you want to do things right from the start. A CPA will help you build the successful habits that will take you from a few properties to a full-blown, rock star empire.

A CPA will help you set up the proper business structure (such as a corporation or LLC), will help you establish proper record-keeping practices so that life will be as easy as possible when tax season rolls around, and will file your taxes every year.

Make sure your CPA has experience with investors. Not every CPA will understand all of the ins and outs of dealing with real estate moguls, and you can save yourself time and headache by dealing with someone who already knows the ropes. And you want someone who is not afraid to be aggressive when it comes to deductions. You have to pay taxes, but you don't need to pay one cent more than the law requires. And that means finding a CPA who will help you legally avoid as many taxes as possible.

153. Should I take out fifteen- or thirty-year mortgages? Which is the better deal?

You should know by now, you can't just throw out a question like that without giving me more facts. The better deal is the one that helps you build your empire as quickly as possible and that gives you the best cash flow. I only do fifteen-year mortgages. I pay more each month, but the properties are paid off sooner, and when they are my cash flow will go through the roof. But in your situation, there may be reasons why it would be better for you to take out thirty-year mortgages. Check with your CPA to make sure which is the best deal for you. Have a long-term plan, and stick to it.

154. What is a direct principal reduction loan?

These are loans offered under the Home Affordable Refinance Program (HARP). There are offered to homeowners, including investors, who own properties secured by loans originated by Fannie Mae or Freddie Mac. The reduction loans are designed for borrowers who have no equity in their properties or are underwater. They can be a great way to refinance properties and eliminate negative cash flow.

155. Do I list my properties' purchase prices or their current values on my financial statements?

Financial statements are snapshots of your current situation. They are designed to let your bank or investors know what you are worth at the present time, and you should list the current values of your properties. However, if a lender asks you for the purchase prices of your properties, make sure you submit that amount. If you are asked for the equity you hold on each property you might also include the purchase price, so that you can document how you arrived at the figure. I like to include current market value to show how much equity I have in my properties.

156. **What's does DBA mean? Should I use that as my business structure?**

DBA stands for "doing business as." It is a legal way of describing the fact that you don't have a formal business structure, such as a corporation or LLC. I don't know of any serious real estate investors who operate as a DBA. Check with your attorney and accountant, but in my opinion you need the legal protection that corporations and LLCs provide. If you own property as a DBA and things go wrong, there may be a lawsuit involved. If your DBA is sued, it may have the same legal effect as suing you as a person. And that could mean that you lose your empire and many of the things you have worked hard to build. Don't take the chance. Set up your company the right way and you will weather many of the storms that will come your way.

However you structure your business, the title company will need to know what name to issue the title under. Double check this. You don't want to realize it was done in the wrong entity's name the day of closing and have to set another date.

157. **What does "taking title" mean?**

Taking title is a fancy way of saying you own the property. You know lawyers. It seems like they charge by the word and don't want to make anything easy. Real estate is one of the few types of property that has a title. When you buy it, your name is added to the list of all the other people who have owned it, and your name is recorded at the county clerk. Everyone who looks at your property will know you own it because when you took title is a matter of public record.

158. **The closer asked what address she should mail the documents to. What documents is she talking about?**

I hope you like paperwork, because when you buy real estate you are going to get a ton of it. On every deal. Stacks of it. Get used to it. If you have mortgages, you will receive multiple documents from the lender.

You may get a note, the copy of the mortgage, and any disclosures that are required by law. You will also need to keep a copy of your loan application. If that is not enough, you will also be given a deed, a bill of sale, a seller's affidavit outlining any known defects to the property, and a buyer/seller settlement statement. You will also see transfer tax declarations and HUD-1 forms. You will need to find a safe place to keep all of those. And be sure to thank your mail carrier. He will haul all of those to you, which not an easy task.

Be sure to have the documents mailed to your business address. In the heat of the moment it can be easy to use the address of the property instead, but that will only cost you a trip to the property to track down your papers.

159. **What does "absolute" mean at an auction?**

When you buy property at an auction, you are given title in fee simple absolute. There are several types of interest you can have in real property, and they all give you different rights and ownership interests. Fee simple absolute is the highest interest you can have. It means you have absolute ownership in the property, and that no one else can claim title. If you die, the property will pass to your estate or heirs. If you hold title under other type of ownership, others may be able to claim an interest in the property when you pass.

160. **If I died, what would happen to my rental properties?**

Not to be too philosophical, but it's not a question of if you will die. It is a question of when. Hopefully, that will be a long time from now, after you have seen your great-grandchildren graduate from college. But it may happen sooner than that. There are no guarantees in life, and we may not make it home today. And that is why you have to visit with your attorney about estate planning.

If you die without a will, your property or the company that owns it will be distributed according to the laws of your state, usually after a long and expensive process. And it may not be distributed how you want it to be. If you have a will, the property or company will be distributed according to the terms of the will. But it will have to go through the process of probate, which is also expensive and time consuming. If you have a trust, all of the property in it will automatically be transferred according to the terms of the trust. There is no probate or court hearing. Although trusts may be more expensive than wills, they might save money over the long-term. And they will make life much easier for your family.

If your business is established as a corporation, review those documents with your attorney. Some articles of incorporation will have provisions that detail what happens if one of the shareholders dies and how that ownership will be transferred. That may impact your estate planning, and you need to take that into account.

161. Can a tenant sue me if she gets carbon monoxide poisoning at one of my properties?

Yes. In fact, there are law firms across the country that are itching to take your money if they think they can prove you are responsible for carbon monoxide poisoning. Attorneys will try to prove that you were negligent, which means that you knew a leak was likely to occur and did nothing about it, or that you did something that caused the leak. They might argue that you allowed exhaust vents to be clogged and didn't clean them. Or they might argue that you installed appliances that you should have known were defective.

Carbon monoxide poisoning can lead to death, and you need to take it seriously. It's another reason you need to inspect your property on a regular basis and make sure everything is functioning properly.

162. **It feels like all of my tenants hate me. How can I keep going?**

Every landlord goes through this. Sometimes, it feels like all of your tenants have banded together and made a secret pact to make your life miserable. They complain about every little detail. If one of the faucets has a tiny leak they hound you until it's fixed. They even blame you for things outside your control, such as a neighbor's dog that barks during the night. When you manage property, you are going to deal with people, and that means you are going to have problems. There will be times when you won't feel appreciated, and you will wonder if it is worth the effort.

Take a long-term view of things and remember that you did not become an investor to win a popularity contest. You did it to build wealth and security for your family. As long as your tenants are paying the rent on time and not tearing up the place, cash the checks and keep your mouth shut.

164. **Everyone in my REIA club says I should use QuickBooks to run my business. Do I have to?**

Part of building an empire is having systems in place to handle your billing, monitoring invoices that have been or need to be paid, and tracking expenses. There are many software programs that allow you to do these things on your computer, smartphone, or tablet. The advantage to using a software package to do this is that all of the information is readily available in one place, and it offers you many different search options. If you want to see all the expenses for a certain property or vendor, you simply type a few keywords into a search box and click. And when April rolls around your CPA will love you because all the information he needs will be on one thumbnail drive.

QuickBooks is one of the most-respected programs for running a business, but it is not the only one. You can chose from many, and need to find one that works for you.

Some people aren't comfortable using computers, especially investors who have been in business for decades. Their system may involve keeping all the receipts in files and handing that off to their accountant at the end of the year. That's not the most efficient system, and it won't work when your business grows. I would recommend they upgrade to a computer system, but as long as they are comfortable using it, that's their choice.

The worst option is to have no system at all. If you can't find your receipts, don't know who has paid rent for the month, or know when you need to pay your bills you are in trouble. Before you buy your first property you should establish a system and be disciplined about using it. That's the savvy way to grow.

164. How do I determine appreciation?

Appreciation is another way of saying how much the value of your property has increased. To determine appreciation, you need to know the value of the property at the time you bought it and its value today. The value at the time you bought it is easy. You can look at the mortgage or the check you wrote.

Determining the current value will be more challenging. You need to pull comps, use online resources such as eppraisal.com, and if you are in a bind hire an appraiser.

Subtract the purchase price from the current value, and the difference is your appreciation. If you bought a house for $50,000 and it's now worth $100,000 it has appreciated $50,000. To determine the rate of appreciation you divide the amount of appreciation by the number of years you have owned the property. If you owned a property for ten years and it appreciated 50 percent, it appreciated at a rate of 5 percent a year.

165. **I have a home office. Am I entitled to a tax deduction?**

You should take every tax deduction you are entitled to. If you don't, you are giving money away. That's right, you are taking food out of the mouths of your children and yanking the clothes off their backs. Consult with your accountant, but home offices generally qualify for a nice tax deduction. It has to be part of the home that is regularly and exclusively used as an office. If you have a desk in your kitchen or bedroom, that may not qualify for the deduction. Also, your home has to be the principle place of your business. And the deduction may be based on the percentage of your home used for the office. If you have the choice between several places in your home for your office, always choose the largest. It will give you the best deduction.

166. **My banker just told me they sold some of my loans to another bank. I don't know the new people and want to keep all of my business at my local bank. Is there any way to prevent this from happening in the future?**

For a while, it seemed like some of my loans were being sold as soon as the ink was dry on the application. It was hard to remember which bank was servicing which loan. Banks sell loans for the same reasons you buy and sell properties: it makes good financial sense. If it is more profitable for a bank to sell a loan than to service it, the loan will probably be sold. It's a headache, but there is nothing you can do about banks selling your loans. If you want to try to play hardball, review your contract and see if it contains an assignability clause. These are the provisions that allow banks to sell loans to other parties. If you have the leverage, maybe you can get your bank to agree to remove any assignability clause. But unless you have enough leverage, such as having an extremely large number of properties or the total value of your loans is large, you probably won't have much luck.

167. **Are closing costs tax deductible?**

Yes. Closing costs are generally treated as expenses in the tax year the property was purchased. Make sure you keep copies of all of the expenses associated with closing and provide them to your accountant.

168. **How do I prevent loss of rent?**

Loss of rent. That phrase makes my skin crawl, gives me migraines, and makes me want to puke. It can mean many things. The first things that come to mind are properties that are ready to rent but aren't occupied by tenants. I lose money every day one of my units is empty. I can avoid that by building a solid marketing plan that lets people know I have great properties to be rented.

Loss of rent also happens when my properties are damaged and cannot be rented. If one of my units suffers fire damage, for example, I won't be able to rent it until the damage is repaired. To avoid this type of loss, visit with your insurance agent about rental loss insurance. A rental loss policy will provide you income while your property is uninhabitable, and will make sure your empire stays safe.

169. **I have two credit cards, and I pay the balance off every month. Do I need to include this in my financial statement?**

A financial statement is designed to give lenders and investors a snapshot of your financial health and the financial health of your company. It contains a list of your assets, liabilities, and your cash flow.

A credit card balance could be construed as a liability, but the liability disappears once you pay the balance. It wouldn't be an asset, and it would certainly show up when you list your cash flow. If you need to explain your credit card use, and you pay off the entire balance each month, the best advice might be to include copies of your three most recent statements. That would give lenders and investors a clear idea of how much money you are running through your credit cards.

The most important advice is to be an open book when lenders ask you about your finances. It's better to provide too much information instead of giving incomplete answers. If there is any question about your credit card balances, give your banker what she needs to feel comfortable.

170. I love being an investor, but as I have added more properties I've found it difficult to take time off. How can I schedule a vacation?

Taking care of yourself is important. If you don't recharge your batteries from time to time you will burn out and your empire will fall apart. As soon as you own enough properties, you need to hire a management company. A management company is responsible for finding tenants, collecting rent, making sure any needed repairs get done, and handling all the other details that come with owning property. With the right management company in place, you can take off as much time as you want. You won't have to feel guilty about not being on site, and you will know that everything will be done.

171. My friends and family like me, and I have a good reputation at work. Will that be enough to get me a loan at the bank?

It would be great to live in a world where everyone was honest and paid his bills on time. But that's not the world we live in, and you know that. Bringing a note to the bank from your mom won't help you. Banks have heard every story in the book. Everyone who fills out a loan application tells them, "I am honest. You can count on me. I will pay off the loan early." Banks do a great job of researching borrowers, but they still have more than enough people who default on loans. Some defaults are caused by significant life events, such as divorce or illness. Others are caused by people who get lazy or indifferent about how they run their businesses. So don't be surprised or offended when your bank asks you to document the details of your life. I know your best friends wouldn't do that, but banks can't afford to take everyone at his word. If they did, it wouldn't be long before the bank examiners showed up and padlocked the front door.

172. **What is a profit and loss statement? Do I need one?**

A profit and loss statement, also known as a P&L or income statement, is a simple form that gives a quick look at the financial health of your business. It lists all of your income and all of your expenses. It's not detailed and only gives the big picture. Many banks will ask for one if you are applying for a loan, and if you are seeking investors it might be a good idea to have one with you as you meet with them. It will be especially important as your empire grows, and you can impress banks with some significant income.

It's simple to make one. Create a form with a space at the top that allows you to record your income. If you have income from more than one source, be sure to include that. Below your income, list your expenses, breaking them done by broad categories, such as mortgage payments, insurance, and utilities. Subtract expenses from income to determine your net income before taxes. The final part of the statement should allow you to indicate your taxes, and then your income after taxes.

Don't overthink the form. Keep it simple. You can find templates online, and don't worry if the entire form is less than one page.

173. **One of my prospective tenants won't move in until I correct all the items on a three-page list she gave me. What should I do? Do you see that?**

Right over your tenant's head. It's a giant red flag, and it means you should proceed with caution. Life with tenants will never get easier when they move in. Life is always easier before they take possession of the property. If someone is difficult before they sign a lease, they will only get more demanding after they sign.

102

If this happens, take a moment to look at the list. Are some of them things that really need to be taken care of? Maybe there are lights that need to be replaced or a leaky faucet you didn't see during your inspection. Look at requests like those as suggestions. The tenant is helping you make your property shine.

But there may be other things that don't need to be done. Maybe the tenant thinks the grass needs to be cut at exactly three-fourths of an inch. Or that the stove needs to be tilted six degrees counterclockwise. Sort the important things that need to be done from the silly requests. If the tenant is not willing to compromise, maybe it's best for her to live somewhere else. If you choose to rent to her, you have given up your right to complain later on. I warned you.

174. Can I tell a tenant to "just move out"?

You can tell tenants lots of things. Tell them that Bigfoot lives in a cave on the other side of the street. Or that they should be careful swimming in the pool late at night because the Loch Ness Monster might show up. But just because you say something doesn't mean it's true or has any merit.

You will have tenants that will make your life miserable, and you will wish you had never met them. I would like to believe that a team of landlords has hired scientists to solve this problem. In a deep cave somewhere near Hogwarts, these scientists are inventing a button that solves the problem of dealing with lousy tenants. All a landlord will have to do is push a button, and all of his tenants will be transported to an alternate dimension. Tenant problems will be solved in an instant.

All kidding aside, you can't wish your bad tenants away, and you should not tell them to just move out. When their lease is up, you can refuse to sign another one with them. Or, if you want to go through the time and hassle, you can evict them, if they have breached their lease.

This is another reason to hire a management company. Pay someone else to deal with tenants. Spend your time putting together deals, watching your children grow up, and holding hands with your wife on the beach.

175. One of my tenants threatened to hurt me. Can I evict her?

It has been known to happen. A tenant complains about a repair that needs to be done, but it doesn't get done quickly enough for the tenant. When the landlord shows up to make the repair, an angry tenant wielding a steak knife chases the landlord off the property.

The easiest way to make sure you have the right to evict the tenant is to have your lease state that threatening behavior is a breach of the lease. Some leases contain a "use and enjoyment clause," which is a broad way of saying that if the tenant does anything that prevents the landlord or other tenants from being able to use the property, the tenant is in breach and can be evicted.

Other states have enacted laws protect tenants from other tenants who brandish weapons. And, if the landlord doesn't do anything about the situation, the other tenants may be allowed to break their leases. The landlord is left with a bunch of empty units.

If a tenant threatens you or another tenant, take the situation seriously. Document everything, and consult with your attorney to know what your options are.

176. The guy who signed one of my leases no longer lives in the property. His girlfriend is the only person living there. How do I get her out?

You're just full of bad news, aren't you?

Hope your luck turns around. You will probably have to evict him and her. He will have to be evicted even if he is not living on the property because he is on the lease. Until you have an order from a judge that says otherwise, he has the right to enter the property. And she may have to be evicted because once she enters the property and starts living there or doing simple things such as receiving her mail there, she may have certain rights.

When it comes to getting people out of your properties, don't take shortcuts. It can be tempting to enter a property and start throwing a deadbeat tenant's stuff or his girlfriend to the street. But tenants have rights, and if you take matters into your own hands you will probably pay for it in the long run. Trying to get rid of tenant or his guest without a court order may bring you serious legal trouble, including being sued for illegal eviction. If the district attorney is really bored, he may even try to have you convicted of theft if the tenant alleges you stole his stuff. Keep your cool, and let the courts take care of getting rid of tenants.

177. **Do I have to provide carbon monoxide detectors?**

At the time I am writing this book, almost half of the states require residential landlords to install detectors. I won't take the time to list them here, in part because other states may change their laws and require them. You should check with your attorney to find out if you are required by law to provide them.

Even if you aren't required by law, you should consider installing carbon monoxide detectors. It's a small investment compared to the price you would pay if someone were to suffer carbon monoxide poisoning on one of your properties. Plus, more states will probably require you to provide detectors in the future, and it may be just a matter of time before you have to install them. It might be a good move to be ahead of the curve.

178. **I heard some investors talking about an expired MSL listing? What is this, and why does it matter to me as an investor?**

The Multiple Listing Service can be a great way to buy and sell properties. It's a database of all the properties listed by a group of real estate agents. If you tell your agent you are looking for property in a certain area, she can run a search of properties in the area that are listed and that are within your price range.

The listing includes the status of the property, including such details as whether it is a new listing or has been sold. An expired listing means that when the agent was hired to sell the property, the contract automatically expired at a certain time. If the property was not sold within six months, for example, the parties were released from their obligations. As a seller, it is savvy to include such a provision. If the deal doesn't work out, you part ways at the end of the deal. This also motivates the agent. If he doesn't sell the property on time, he doesn't make a commission.

179. How do I find a good roofer that guarantees his work?

Thank you for this question. I needed a good laugh. I wish I had the answer. Let me begin by telling you what you shouldn't do. I live in Oklahoma, and we often have tornados and hailstorms in the spring. In bad years, many houses need new roofs. When that happens, roofers from all over the place descend on us. There is no way to know where they are from, if they do good work, or if they have ever even completed one project. Never hire a roofer who has rolled into town after a natural disaster.

One of the best ways to find a good roofer (or electrician or plumber) is to ask other investors. You may have to use a crowbar to pry names out of them, but the ones you get will probably be good. Once you find a good roofer, do everything you can to keep him around. Bring him coffee, cupcakes, and buckets of water. Send his wife flowers on their wedding anniversary. Do whatever it takes to keep him satisfied because good roofers are hard to find.

180. Do you pay a roofer before the work is started?

You have a great sense of humor. Pay a roofer before he starts? What's next, handing my credit cards to strangers on the street? Are you crazy?

Never, ever, ever pay a roofer before he starts. In fact, I almost never pay anyone in advance. I've been burned too many times to let that happen again. The only time I pay people in advance is when they have worked with me before, and I know that they will do the work I hired them to do. And they need to offer me a discount for being paid up front.

Any quality roofer will not expect to be paid up front. Local roofers with a proven track record will have credit accounts with suppliers, and they won't even ask to be paid for materials until the job is done. Be wary of any roofer, plumber, or electrician who needs to be paid in advance. You may be giving your money away.

181. If I install new roofs, will my insurance premiums be lowered?

Property owners in Oklahoma learn a lot about roofing. We have installed quite a few of them over the years. In some places, your insurance company will reduce your premiums if you upgrade your roof. You may be entitled to a discount if you install impact resistant shingles. If you live in an area prone to hurricanes, you may be entitled to a discount by using wind mitigation methods. And in other places you might be entitled to a discount if you install flame retardant material. Check with your insurance company to find out what discounts you can receive, and take advantage of those when you have to replace a roof.

182. I think it's time to raise the rent on one of my properties, but the long-standing tenant says he can't afford it. What should I do?

My natural instinct is to turn the guy upside down and see what falls out of his pockets. Hopefully, it's gobs and gobs of cash. This is a tough call. If he has been a good tenant and paid his rent on time, I would do as much as I could to keep him in my property. Of course, you don't want to take a beating on the difference in rent. Think about how much it costs to find a new tenant. Factor in the risk they won't be as good as the old one. Do you feel the increased rent payment is enough to offset the risk of finding and having a new tenant?

183. **What is "cash for keys," and is it worth it?**

Cash for keys can be one of the best ways to deal with problem tenants. If you use it properly, it can save you time and eliminate headaches. Suppose a tenant falls behind on his rent or becomes such a nuisance to deal with that you want to get rid of him immediately. The law won't allow you to do anything until he is evicted or his lease expires.

But evictions cost time and money, and they can be frustrating. One of the best ways to eliminate those things is to offer the client cash to move out. You give him cash, and he returns his keys. It's that simple. You don't have to file anything at the courthouse or hire a lawyer. Your problem is solved, and you can get your property ready to rent to another tenant.

If you pay someone to move out, make sure you get the agreement in writing. You don't want the tenant saying you tossed him out on the street for no reason. And I would pay by check. You want a nice fat paper trail to cover your backside.

184. **I am considering investing in real estate, but I don't like dealing with people. Is that going to be a problem?**

It might be. If the idea of dealing with people makes your skin crawl, you might want to look for another place to invest. When you buy your first properties, you will have to interact with your tenants. It won't be cost effective to hire a management company, and you need the experience of dealing with tenants. This is one of the best ways to learn the industry, even if it drives you crazy. When you have enough properties to hire a company to manage them, you will understand what the managers are dealing with and whether they are bluffing you when they give you updates.

185. **One of my tenants calls me every other day with petty complaints. What should I do?**

Get ready for this. A tenant will sign a lease, and you will think she is the greatest person ever. She is warm, inviting, and funny. And then, as soon as she unpacks her last box, she is possessed by Satan. Nothing is good enough for her. She doesn't like the carpet. The windows don't face the right direction. The water isn't cold enough, and she wants you to fix it. NOW. Tenants like this will frustrate you to death. It will take you a phone call or two to understand when there are legitimate concerns about the property and when a tenant is just difficult. Regardless of how stringent your screening process is, a few difficult ones will slip past and make their way into your life.

Once it becomes clear that the tenant is the problem, you need to meet them face to face and set expectations. The tenant needs to understand you are not there to cater to her every whim. You have a business to run and other units to manage. Be polite but firm, and stay calm. Let her know you are not going to respond to any more calls that don't involve matters outlined in the lease. If that doesn't solve the problem, document the calls and send a copy of the list to the tenant. Include a brief but accurate description of what you did. If nothing else, you will have proof of all the silly calls she made to you and how you responded. If you have to evict her or refuse to renew her lease you will have ammo to defend yourself against a discrimination or harassment lawsuit.

You also want to make sure you are operating from a position of power and not weakness. If you don't understand the laws and regulations of renting property, you will be at a distinct disadvantage. Some of the tenants you deal with will be very savvy about landlord/tenant law. We call them "professional tenants." They may know more than you. They may understand what you can and cannot do, and once they know you are trying to bluff your way through a situation you are done. They will smell blood in the water and start circling. Don't let this happen. Make sure you are the expert on landlord/tenant law and not your tenants.

186. **I need some cash. I have equity in my residence. Should I borrow against that and use the funds to build my business?**

No. Just thinking about that makes me nervous. There will be times when you need to inject cash into your business. It doesn't matter how small or large your empire is. There will be times when your cash flow isn't what it should be and you need to find a way to improve it. But you should never borrow against your home. Your home should be your sanctuary, the place you can go and spend time loving your family. It's the place where you and your loved ones enjoy the fruits of all of your hard work and where you dream and plan for the future.

If you leverage your home, it will only put undue stress on you and your family. If your business doesn't turn around, you won't worry about just saving the business. You will worry about how to pay the additional debt on your home.

The goal is to build enough cash flow to pay off your mortgage. You want the security of owning a home free and clear. You don't want to create additional debt that may not give you the tax benefits a business loan would and that might put you in a situation where you lose the most valuable and precious possession you own.

187. **There are several banks in my area that lend to investors. Should I use one or several of them to finance my deals?**

The key to good financing is the interest rate. If you deal with only one bank, you get to know the loan officers and what they expect. You develop relationships over time, and those relationships will help you get deals done. The bank knows you and knows you are good for the loan. But as your company grows, you may be able to leverage your position by shopping around at different banks. If you have enough properties, you may be such an attractive prospect, banks are willing to waive fees and lower interest rates. That means money in your pocket. If you really hit the big time, your empire may become so big you outgrow your original bank and are forced to look at other options. When that happens, don't settle for the first offer that comes along. Make sure to get the best deal possible, even if it means you let two lenders bid against each other.

188. Should I borrow money from my rich relatives?

Here are a few ideas that are better than doing business with family: swimming in shark-infested waters in a bathing suit made of bloody beef, wearing pants made of sixty-grit sandpaper, or letting your buddy practice his hammering skills on your fingers.

Borrowing money from relatives is like trying to hug a rattlesnake. You know it's going to bite you, you just don't know when. I don't care how much money they have, you will regret doing business with family. Something will go wrong, and instead of dealing with it in a calm, professional manner, feelings will come into play and rational decision-making will go out the window.

189. What documents should I bring when I meet with a bank to borrow money?

Your bank will give you a list of the information it needs. Do yourself a favor and bring them everything they ask for. You don't want to get to the bank and have to reschedule your meeting or have your application denied because you weren't prepared. You should expect to bring two year's worth of W-2s and tax returns or detailed financial information if you are self-employed. And if you have other sources of income, such as alimony, child support, or retirement, you need to bring documentation of that as well. Even if the bank doesn't specifically ask for it, bring any paperwork you think will make you look like a more attractive borrower. Put yourself in a position to succeed.

190. Is an investment home loan the same as a personal residence home loan or a commercial loan?

No. Banks handle the loans differently, and there may be different tax consequences for each. An investment loan will be handled by the lender's business department. In addition to reviewing your credit history (or the credit history of any of the other officers of your corporation), the bank will analyze your business model and the risks associated with it. You can improve your chances of having your business loan approved by having a track record of deals that have worked, and by showing how other investors have been able to run successful businesses in your area. Most lenders will have residential loan departments, and they will review your credit, your job history, and sift through all of your financial documents. Lenders will also have commercial loan departments, and in addition to reviewing your credit history, they will analyze your business and how likely you are to make a profit.

191. How come some banks loan money for investors to purchase rental properties, and others don't?

All banks are not created equal. They frequently specialize, and some focus on residential loans. Some will loan money for residential investors, and others will loan money for commercial properties. The larger the bank is, the more likely it is to loan money for all types of projects. Understanding what your bank offers and learning how to capitalize on that will make your life as an investor much easier. If you don't have a bank yet, ask fellow investors where they bank. Visit with the bank that handles your home mortgage and your checking accounts. If they don't loan for investment property, they probably know a lender that does.

192. I just came back from vacation, and I loved the place I visited. I am thinking about buying property there next week. Is that a good idea?

You should never invest your hard earned money if you don't understand the local market. I am all for expanding your empire, but you have to be savvy about it. Research the area before you write a check. Make sure you know what the property values are and where the most desirable parts of town are. What is the average rent? Take your time, do your due diligence, and you will make wise investment choices.

193. Dave Ramsey says that some bankers are lazy and only look at your FICO score, while others do "actual underwriting" and look at your entire financial situation to qualify you. How do I find a banker like that?

Most bankers will look at your entire application to decide whether or not you are a good risk. However, your FICO score is an important part of your application, and most lenders place a lot of weight on it. If your score is too low, you may be fighting an uphill battle with many banks. You may be given the chance to explain rough spots in your credit, but it's best to take care of those before you apply for a loan. If you have old debt that shows up on your credit report, take care of it as soon as you can. Even if you are approved with a low FICO, you will be charged a higher interest rate. The money you save by taking care of old debt will make it worth your while.

194. Rich Dad says your credit score doesn't matter if you have a "financial statement." Is that true? What is a financial statement, and how do I get one?

The Rich Dad series has changed thousands of lives and sold millions of copies. The impact of those books will be felt for decades. Rich Dad, Poor Dad changed my life and is one of the reasons I became an investor. So I don't disagree with its author lightly. Your credit score always matters. It is an important piece of the puzzle when you are trying to secure financing.

Financial statements are documents that show the health of a business. There are two primary parts to a financial statement, the balance sheet and the income statement. The balance sheet shows what the business owns and what it owes. It lists the assets, liabilities and net worth of any assets, and equity in any property. The income statement, also called a profit and loss statement, shows the business' income and expenses over a given period. You can draft a financial statement yourself. There are templates available online. If you create a financial statement on your own, make sure it looks as professional as possible. Don't omit anything, even if it makes you look bad. It's better to be known as a businessman who had some challenges as opposed to a liar.

You might want to invest in an accountant preparing the statement. It may cost a few dollars, but you will have a professional document that you can present to any investor or lender with pride. An accountant will verify the information you give him, and may sign off on the accuracy of the report. That will give you instant credibility and should increase your chances of being approved for a loan.

195. I've heard that it's hard to get financing if you are trying to buy a property through an LLC. Is that true?

No. Most properties are bought through some type of business structure, such as an LLC or a corporation. It is so common if you didn't do it your lender might give you an odd look, and I wouldn't recommend doing business without the legal protection of an LLC or corporation. The lender will look at the LLC's history, the credit of the officers, and make a decision based on that. The fact that you are using an LLC will show you are an astute business person and trying to grow your business the right way.

196. Can I transfer a property into an LLC if I owe money on it?

Yes. An LLC can own property whether it has liens on it or not. In fact, most of the property you own should have liens on it. Never purchase property outright with your money when you can borrow other people's money. That helps you leverage your business and allows you to take advantage of all of the tax deductions that come with paying interest on business loans.

197. Is it better to use banks or credit unions?

You should use whichever lender loans you the most money at the best interest rate. As far as your business is concerned, there is not much difference between a credit union and a traditional bank. They offer many of the same services, and if your credit union works for you, stay with them.

The key distinction is that credit unions are owned by its customers, also called members. Banks are often owned by shareholders who are more concerned about the profitability of the bank. Another important issue is that many credit unions don't have the assets that many banks have, especially the larger banks. That may limit their ability to lend larger sums of money.

198. Is it better to use a brick-and-mortar bank or an online bank?

Again, you should use whichever bank gives you the best opportunity to build your empire. Online banks are growing in popularity, especially for consumers who like the convenience of banking from home and who don't need or like to deal with bankers face to face. I don't use online banking for my loans because they currently don't have the resources to loan the amounts of money I need. But my preferences may change over time.

199. Should I use a small local bank or a large national bank like Bank of America?

You know this by now. Use whichever bank can help you grow your empire. When you start, your best option will be to borrow from small community banks that loan commercial money to real estate investors. Talk with a vice-president and make sure the bank has $150,000,000 in assets or less.

But your goal should be to grow such a giant empire your local bank can't meet your needs. You want to outgrow the local guys and start playing with the big boys. You want to be such a player that when you call a senior loan officer at one of the largest banks in the country, he returns it as soon as he is done with his meeting. If you're going to dream, dream big. Don't waste your time thinking small. You will thank me later.

200. **What is a mortgage broker?**

A mortgage broker is someone who connects borrowers with lenders. You will want to meet a good mortgage broker. They don't lend money. They find non-traditional lenders who are looking to lend their money to real estate investors. The brokers collect the information from the borrower and pass it to potential lenders. If the lenders approve the loan, the broker is paid an origination fee. Brokers can be a great source of cash for your business, and you should seek out one or two in your area.

201. **If I have terrible credit can I still own rental properties?**

Yes, but it will make it more difficult to start your empire. Your credit score will have a huge impact on your business. It will determine whether or not you qualify for loans, what interest rate you pay, and how much you are charged for insurance. But it won't make it impossible for you to build a great portfolio. Many investors get into the business because they tried other ventures that didn't pan out.

Having bad credit should be your inspiration to find great deals today. The faster you buy properties, rehab them, and rent them out, the faster you will start cash flowing. And the faster you cash flow, the faster you can rebuild your credit.

Even if you have made mistakes in the past, you can take steps today that will improve your tomorrow. Learn from your mistakes, pay off past bills, and move forward.

Another great opportunity is to look for owner-finance deals. When investors retire, they often want to sell properties and are willing to carry the note. They will be savvy, and if you don't know what you are doing you may take a beating. You have been warned.

202. **I owe money on rental properties. Will that make it hard for me to get a loan for a house?**

Let's clarify one thing. As a general rule, you should never own invest-ment property in your name. Talk with your attorney and your accoun-tant to see what structure works best for you, but all serious investors buy, sell, and own property through a corporation, LLC, or similar business structure.

If you have your business structured properly, the debt of the business and your personal debt will be two separate issues. That's important, because one of the factors used to determine your credit score is your debt to income ratio. The lower the ratio, the better. If your ratio is high, you will be seen as a high risk. Lenders will charge you a higher interest rate, and it may be harder for you to be approved. If you own your investment properties in your name, the value of the debt will be counted against your debt to income ratio, and you want to avoid that. Generally, your debt payments should not exceed 36 percent of your gross monthly income.

203. **Should I have a separate loan on each property or consolidate them?**

Consolidate them as soon as you can. And when you have the chance, borrow money in large blocks. It's much easier to borrow $400,000 than it is to borrow $40,000 ten times.

Consolidation will make your life easier. You will only have one pay-ment to make each month instead of dozens, and you won't have to endure the headache, frustration, and multiple fees of applying for mul-tiple loans.

204. I have been studying real estate investing for some time, and I am confused. Robert G. Allen says I should buy property with nothing down and finance as much as I can. Dave Ramsey says to avoid debt and pay cash. Who am I supposed to believe?

There are many opinions when it comes to building your empire. Allen and Ramsey are two successful investors, and they have completely different approaches. You have to find what works for you. I believe in the power of leveraging money. You want to finance your purchases using other people's money, and you want to take advantage of all the tax deductions you receive when you borrow money. Leveraging money has allowed me to build my empire more quickly than I could have done on my own, and I don't regret doing it and will do it in the future.

But the goal is to pay off the debt and reap the benefits of high cash flow. When I own my properties outright, I will cash flow like a rock star. Then, if I choose, I can borrow more money to buy more properties.

205. What kind of bank account should I keep people's security deposits in?

Security deposits are a double-edged sword. On one hand, they let me sleep easy at night. I know that if one of my tenants damages my property I can recover at least some of the cost of the repairs.

On the other hand, they can be difficult to keep track of. They can cause problems if you don't know how to handle them. This is another area that differs greatly from state to state. In some places, you have to keep security deposits in a bank account separate from any other funds, and you may have to pay interest to the tenant when the deposit is returned. If you try to offset any damages or back rent against a security deposit, the level of written documentation you have to provide may vary as well. Consult with your attorney and understand what you can and cannot do.

But here is one thought you should have whenever you accept a security deposit. Security deposits are not an income stream. You cannot take security deposits and use them to finance a vacation to the South Pacific. Security deposits are a liability. If you don't handle them properly, you may wind up paying your tenants the deposit and fines. Always account for the deposits in the way your state requires. The best way is to deposit them into a special account where nothing else is deposited.

Be careful with security deposits. Treat them like hand grenades. You don't want them exploding in your face.

206. I own property through an LLC. Do I need to do my banking any differently?

Yes. This may not make sense, but an LLC is a legal person. It has its own identity, rights, and responsibilities. Part of owning and managing an LLC the right way is to open a bank account under the LLC's name and deposit the rent checks you earn from property owned by the LLC into the account. If you don't, you may lose the tax deductions and liability protection you receive from owning an LLC.

207. Why do some banks loan 80 percent on rental properties while other only loan 70 percent?

Most lenders, especially hard-money lenders (those that expect repayment within six months to a year) will not issue loans for the full value of investment properties. They typically will not loan more than 70 or 80 percent of the properties after repaired value (ARV). When making a loan, lenders have to take into consideration the costs associated with foreclosing on a property, as well as the anticipated costs of repairing it. If lenders agree to loan 90 percent on properties and the borrower defaults, banks could lose money trying to get the property ready for resale. These numbers weren't picked at random. Banks have compiled years and years of information and found that 70 to 80 percent is the loan value that gives them the best chance to remain profitable. The percentage that a bank chooses will factor in the needed repairs and the relationship or credit rating of the borrower.

208. **As long as my property is rented, I can make the payment. But what if the property is vacant? How will I pay my mortgage?**

Here is a little tip from Business 101. Every business has to have enough customers to make a profit. Regardless of whether you are a dentist, own an ice cream parlor, or rent properties, if you don't have enough people paying for your services or product you will soon be out of business.

Here are two solid ways to make sure you can survive slow times in your business. First, develop a marketing plan. If people don't know you have houses to rent they can't sign leases and write you checks every month. And if your marketing plan works like it should, you will have tenants lined up to rent from you when you have a vacancy.

The second thing you need to do is to establish an emergency savings fund for each property. You need to have enough cash on hand to weather the tough times you will face. I recommend having enough cash to pay the mortgage and expenses for three months on each property. If you aren't able to rent one of your properties that will give you a cushion and you won't have to worry about how the mortgage is going to be paid. That sounds like a lot of money, but it's a small price to pay for your peace of mind.

209. **What happens to my loans if I die?**

May you live for decades after your loans are paid off, and may you bask in the joy of your massive cash flow!

What happens to your outstanding loans will depend on your level of planning. Loans, especially those secured by real estate, will not fade away when you die. If you don't do any planning, what is likely to happen after you die is the properties will be foreclosed on when your company can't afford to make the payments. Your family won't have the income you created for them.

You should have some type of succession plan that addresses what happens to your company in the event of your death. It sounds morbid, but no one lives forever. You can't hide from that, especially if you have a family to take care of. With proper planning, someone else will be given the power to control the company. That person will be responsible for making mortgage payments on time. The business will run as if you never left.

You should also have enough life insurance to cover the value of your debts. If you die, the proceeds can be used to pay off the debt. Your family can run the business and enjoy the fruits of your labor.

210. How do I rebuild my credit score?

Many people go through tough times, and we don't all have perfect credit. Regardless of what has happened in your past, you can take steps today that will improve your score in the future. Some people sell services that claim if you pay them they can wave a magic wand over your FICO and make everything go away. Don't waste your money. There are things you can do to repair damaged credit, but it's not as simple as writing a check. It takes time and discipline.

Don't keep making the same mistakes that caused the problem. Don't carry a high balance on your credit cards, which is another way of saying keep the ratio of debt to available credit low. Pay your bills on time. Pay off debt. Don't apply for or open a bunch of new credit accounts. Manage the credit you have responsibly. If you take those steps, over time your credit score will improve.

You should also pull your credit report and contest any inaccurate dings you find. Notify the major credit agencies of any mistakes you find, document them and stay in contact with the agencies until they are removed.

211. **How do I get a loan for a property in another state?**

I love this question. It makes me think that you are dreaming big and that you want your empire to stretch from coast to coast.

Getting a loan for property in another state may be the easy part. You will need to find a lender that is willing to loan in the area where the property is located. If you are using a small bank located in your home state, this might be a challenge. They might not be familiar with the regulations and laws in the second state. Even small things such as how to record a lien or file a mortgage can vary from state to state, and lenders may be wary of trying to place a lien on a property if they aren't comfortable with how laws work in the state where the property is located. If you do business with a large bank, such as Chase or Bank of America, this will present less of a problem. They have branches throughout the country. You also have the option of finding a bank in the same state as the property. You will be starting as a brand new customer and will have to document your success in your home state. Be prepared to prove every cent you earn.

The bigger issue with buying property out of state is understanding landlord/tenant law in that state. Handling things such as evictions and security deposits can be completely different, and if you fail to meet the requirements the consequences can be severe. Make sure you visit with an attorney in the new state and understand your rights and responsibilities before you buy your first property in another state.

212. **How do I know when it's time to refinance?**

It's time to refinance when the numbers add up. You should know what the interest rate on your current mortgage is, and if your bank offers you a lower rate that justifies the time and expense of refinancing, you should consider doing it. You need to understand the fees associated with refinancing and how it impacts your portfolio and long-term goals.

You shouldn't refinance just to do it. It has to make sense from a financial point of view, and you won't know that unless you take a detailed look at the numbers.

Consider the fees and the savings to see how long it would take to cover your costs. If the refinance costs you $5,000 in fees and costs and you save $500 per month, it will take ten months to get your money back. If you find a deal like that, consider taking it.

213. Can you buy properties from banks? How do I do that?

Yes, you can buy properties from banks, and you should consider adding as many of those properties as you can. Banks will typically offer two types of properties. One type is foreclosures, where the owner could no longer make the payments on the property and was unable to sell it or to negotiate a different arrangement with the bank. Banks will often advertise foreclosure properties, and if you keep your ear to the ground at your REIA club meetings you may hear about them. You may also see signs on properties saying that the property will be sold at auction.

Another type of sale you will see banks offer is a "short sale." If a borrower can no longer afford his mortgage and owes more than the property is worth, the bank may sell it at a loss. It is cheaper and quicker to do that than it to foreclose on the property, and if you do your due diligence you can find bargains on properties.

If you are feeling aggressive, call the asset manager at your bank to see if they have any underperforming assets. Let them know you would love to help them with those. You never know what will happen.

214. I just found the perfect house. I look at it and I hear birds singing. I imagine children playing on a swing set in the backyard. It's such a beautiful place I am going to buy it regardless of the price. I know I can charge whatever I want and people will line up to pay it. What do you think?

Take a breath and step away from your checkbook. Never become emotionally attached to a property. Investment property should be about numbers, and the only reason you buy a property is because it makes financial sense. If you are negotiating for a property is because it makes you feel warm and fuzzy, go back to your office and take a nap. The feeling will pass, and your common sense will return.

215. How late can I be on a payment before it shows up on my credit?

You should never be late on a payment. Keeping your credit healthy is very import. You won't be able to build an empire without good credit. But things happen, and you may find yourself in a situation where you can't make a payment on time.

Different lenders have different policies, but a good rule of thumb is that any payments over thirty days past due will be reported to a credit agency. If you anticipate a problem making payments on time, don't bury your head in the sand. Talk to the lender and see if you can make a partial payment. Ask what options you have. You want to guard your credit score. It is your key to the kingdom.

216. Is it possible to negotiate interest rates with a bank?

Yes, and you should negotiate on everything. The key is finding leverage. When you only own one or two properties, you don't have much leverage. Banks don't have an incentive to give you a break because you are a small fish. But as your company grows, banks will want to keep you as a customer. You will gain power and will be able to ask for and receive terms you couldn't when your business was small.

And when you get really big, banks will start competing for your business. You will be able to have them bid against each other, and that's when you can save real money.

Interest rates aren't the only things you should be negotiating. Always discuss fees and costs. If you can reduce those you will save a bundle over the life of your investing career.

217. **Are ARMs ever a good idea?**

Adjustable rate mortgages (ARMs) differ from traditional loans in that the interest rate on an ARM may fluctuate. They are also known as variable-rate mortgages, and the rate can be adjusted periodically based on how much it costs the lender to borrow money.

ARMs can work, but you have to be prepared for an increase in your mortgage payments. You have to anticipate and plan for the most expensive payment you can have. Many borrowers see the low payment in ARMs. They think the rate will always be low. When the rate increases, they are not prepared. The new numbers completely destroy their business model. If you borrow money using an ARM, be sure to calculate your costs at the highest interest rate. Don't let factors out of your control ruin your business.

218. **I'm a pretty good judge of character. When prospective tenant walks into the office, my gut tells me whether I should rent to her or not. Why should I waste my time screening tenants I feel good about?**

I'm a big believer in trusting your gut. Your instincts will guide you in the right direction more often than not. But you shouldn't rely on your gut alone. Get as much information as you can before you decide whether or not you will rent to someone.

And you need to apply your screening process fairly. Everyone should be treated the same, and you need to be able to prove you treat everyone the same. Only screening some tenants leaves you open to claims of discrimination, and that can take a bite out of your company. Have a process to screen clients and use it every time.

219. **My bank just denied my loan application. What do I do now?**

This happens to almost every investor at some point. Don't let it get you down. Look at it as a learning opportunity, and get as much information as you can. When you are denied for a loan, you should receive written notice as to why the lender made its decision. Take that to heart and correct whatever problems you can. You should also visit with the loan officer who handled your application. Ask as many questions as you can. Information is power, and if you know what the issues are you will know what to correct. What you shouldn't do is to let the setback get in the way of you building your empire.

220. I've heard that it's hard to get a loan on a property with roof or foundation issues. Is that true?

Many of the properties I buy are in rough shape. They need roof repair, foundation work, or plumbing and electrical work. Banks know the kinds of properties investors buy, and they have factored that into the mortgages they offer. I don't have trouble finding loans for my properties, and you shouldn't either. However, banks generally won't loan more than 70 percent of the after-rehab value of properties. They protect themselves by only loaning a fraction of the money the property is worth.

221. I found a house at a bargain price, but it needs $20,000 worth of repairs. How do I get the financing for the rehab?

Your offer on any property should take into account the costs of any repairs. You need to have a strong sense of what needs to be done and what it will cost. You also need to know what similar properties in the area rent and sell for. When you crunch the numbers, your offer should not be more than 60 to 70 percent of the after-repaired value. That's as much as most banks will loan on investment property.

There are some companies that will loan you 100 percent of the purchase price of the house and rehab costs, up to 60 or 65 percent of the after-repaired value. Some of them advertise they will pay 100 percent of the house cost at closing, and the funds for repairs will be put in escrow and paid out as needed. I have never used these services and can't tell you if they are worth the costs or not. But there are other options investors should consider.

The most powerful way to pay for rehab expenses is to understand your market and to negotiate the right price for the property. Your final offer should account for the cost of repair. The combined amount should not exceed 70 percent of the after-repaired value.

222. Somebody told me that "remodeling" a house and "repairing" a house have different tax consequences. They sound the same to me. Is there really a difference?

Yes. It may not make sense to you, but to all the tax attorneys and lobbyists who "help" Congress draft the tax code, there can be a big difference. Thinking about how our tax system works gives me a headache, and you should talk with your accountant about these issues if you have any questions.

Here is the simple, layman's answer. The distinction is whether your actions add long-term value to the property (which are classified as capital expenditures) or whether they just keep the property in good condition, such as painting the property or repairing a torn window screen. Capital expenses include such things as replacing a roof or adding a pool.

The IRS may treat capital improvements as investments. They aren't treated as expenses, and you may be able to claim depreciation over time. Repairs, which don't increase the value of the property, may be treated as expenses, and these may be subtracted from your total income. This may reduce your tax liability for the year the expenses were incurred.

223. Would you ever take out a second mortgage on a property?

No. First mortgages allow me to buy investment property. They help me make money that I could not make without the loan. Second mortgages, however, don't create any additional revenue. The monthly payment is an additional expense, and the result is taking equity out of the property and putting it somewhere else. First mortgages are opportunities. Second mortgages are unnecessary drains on your income.

224. I can't make heads or tails of loan papers. Should I hire a lawyer to look them over?

As an investor, you will have plenty of chances to hand your hard earned money over to lawyers. You will pay them to draft agreements, to do title work, and to sue and evict tenants. Don't give them one more penny than you have to.

If you hire an attorney to review the paperwork every time you take out a loan you will go broke. You need to learn how to review all the paperwork you will see as an investor. You should be able to read a mortgage and understand the important terms and what the clauses mean. Don't let that intimidate you. Most of the mortgages you read will be almost identical. You will learn what passages are truly important and what passages don't matter. When you learn to read legal documents, you educate yourself. At the same time, you save hundreds or thousands of dollars in legal fees.

225. A friend of mine is a successful investor, but he owes millions of dollars on his properties. Just the thought of it gives me nightmares. How much debt is okay?

You should never take out more debt than you are comfortable with. Investing in anything is a risk, and there are no guarantees. You may lose money investing in real estate. Some people are naturally risk adverse. They prefer the safety and comfort of not taking chances. The good news is they will never suffer a big loss. But the bad news is they will never have any big wins. To be successful, you have to be willing to take risks, and that may mean taking out business debt.

There is another way to look at your friend's situation. Those millions of dollars purchased millions of dollars' worth of real estate. And that real estate is generating positive cash flow each and every month. And as long as your friend takes care of the property and his tenants, his investments will earn income for years to come. I like those odds, and the risk isn't too much for me.

226. If things go bad and I can't pay the mortgages on my investment properties is there a way to shield my home and my spouse from the consequences?

Yes. Part of building a successful empire is to start with a plan that protects you in the event your business does not grow as you planned. As you should know by now, I believe every investor should visit an attorney and CPA before he buys his first property. One of the things you should discuss is what business structure you should use. If you establish a corporation or LLC and use that structure to operate your business, you will shield yourself and those around you from the liability of a failed business venture.

In many places, your home may be protected from creditors. Even if someone sues you and wins, they cannot put a lien on your home or seize it. It's often called a homestead exemption. The exemption won't protect your home from everything. If you don't pay your mortgage, income taxes, or child support you could risk losing your home. Be savvy, and visit with your attorney about whether or not your state allows a homestead exemption.

227. I was just approved for a loan, but I have to come up with a down payment. Will the bank care if I borrow it from another source?

Your bank will care for two reasons. The additional debt will change your debt to income ratio, and they may want to review your application again and see if you still fit within their credit guidelines. The second reason the bank will care is that the second lender will probably want to secure the debt by placing a lien on the property. This may interfere with your bank's ability to claim clear title, and they will want to know about the other lender. Don't withhold information from any of your lenders. At the least, you will come across as dishonest. At worst, you could be charged with fraud. Don't put yourself in that position.

228. What are wraparound mortgages? Should I avoid them?

Real estate investors use the term "wraparound mortgage" differently than bankers or lenders. To us, it's a good way to finance people who have rough credit or who couldn't get financed through a traditional lender. With a wraparound mortgage, the seller allows the buyer to take possession of the property while the buyer makes payments. The seller keeps title, and the bank is not notified of the transaction. The title never changes hands until it's paid off. And if the buyer defaults, you keep the property, the down payments, and all the payments the buyer made, and get to sell the property again.

229. How do I build a personal relationship with a banker?

Relationships are built over time, and take trust and honesty. The best way to build a personal relationship with your banker is to be a good customer. Pay your loans on time. When you have an appointment to discuss a loan, have your paperwork ready. Prepare professional financial documents. Instead of zipping through the drive-through lane to make a deposit, take a few extra minutes, use the teller in the lobby, and visit with your banker in his office. And once or twice a year, invite your banker to lunch. If he accepts, you can spend time with him and get to know each other. Even if he doesn't accept, he will remember the gesture.

Treat your banker with the respect and decency you want. Over time, you will develop a relationship. And that will help your business grow. And you might make a friend in the process.

230. How much of the mortgage interest can I write off?

I know you are tired of hearing this, but you should check with your accountant about this issue. Don't rely on what a landlord like me says. But mortgage interest is one of the biggest deductions landlords have. You can deduct all of the interest you pay on mortgages for rental properties. If you don't, you are leaving money on the table.

231. Should I make minimum payments or try to pay my properties off as soon as possible?

Your goal as a landlord is to pay off your loans so that your cash flow goes crazy. You want as much money coming in as possible and as little as possible being paid out to banks. What's left over goes right into your pockets.

But that doesn't mean you should pay off every mortgage early. If you do, you may lose your deduction for interest on the mortgages, and that will impact your bottom line. Also, it will take cash out of your business. And you need cash on hand to cover unexpected expenses. Plus, if you need to apply for another loan, having a nice fat pile of cash in the bank will make you a much more attractive client.

232. How do I get the lowest possible interest rate?

Make sure your credit is clean. Pull a copy of your report, and make sure you haven't forgotten about some debt that is listed. If there are problems, take care of them. One of the most significant factors in determining the interest rates for your loans will be your credit score. Take care of it. A few points in the wrong direction can cost you serious cash.

Negotiate. Everything is negotiable, especially when it comes to banks. If you have been a good customer with a long history of making payments on time, you can leverage that into lower interest rates. Don't be afraid to ask. And don't be afraid to look at the interest rates other banks would offer you. You don't have to switch banks and give up your long relationship with yours. But if there is a lower rate somewhere else, use that to your advantage.

233. Will a banker ever ask for additional collateral?

Yes. If you are seen as a high-risk investment, you may be asked to give the bank something extra to make the deal happen. Sometimes this will be in the form of a larger down payment. Other times you may be asked for a security interest in other rental properties you own. Avoid this possibility by making sure you are the best applicant you can be.

234. How important is an ROI and should I worry about the first year returns?

Return on investment (ROI) is an important indicator of whether or not a property is a good investment. ROI is determined by dividing the net income by the cash used to purchase the property. The higher the ROI, the better the investment.

But you need to be careful when looking at your ROI, because the numbers can fluctuate depending on how deals are set up. And this can impact your cash flow. The less cash you put in a deal, the higher your ROI will be. But your net income will be lower because you will be paying a higher mortgage. So always look at more than the ROI if you want to get a clear picture of the investment.

You should worry about every year's return. Don't take anything for granted.

235. What is "legal consideration"?

Consideration is the value each party gives to a contract. If I agree to buy a property for $40,000 my consideration is the money. Your consideration is the property. Both parties have to give legal consideration or the contract will not be enforceable.

In real estate investing, examples of consideration include making a down payment and paying earnest money.

236. What does "emerging markets" mean?

You may not hear the phase "emerging markets" unless you invest in properties overseas. The term refers to countries that are somewhat developed, but are not on par with fully developed countries such as the United States or Japan. As an investor, emerging markets create opportunities because as the economy grows the demand for goods and services increases. It's an opportunity for you to buy low and sell high.

In real estate investing, it means areas that are becoming hot. Places where property hasn't been desirable it the past but where you can make money now and in the future.

237. How can I protect myself from a crash or have success in a boom? The best way to protect yourself from a crash is to understand the market cycle. Where are property prices now? Are they high, or are they low?

If you buy properties when prices are at their highest and the cycle turns, you may never be able to rent the properties and generate positive cash flow. Cycles will impact rental rates, and if your business model is based on rents you could charge only when property is hot, you may be in trouble when the market turns.

Success in a boom will come naturally if you learn the lessons in the book The Savvy Landlord and apply them. You need to buy low, set your rents appropriate for your area, and make sure you have the right tenants. Crunch the numbers before you sign on the dotted line, and don't carry more debt than you can handle. If you build a solid base, you can handle anything.

238. **The only properties I own are multi-family. How can I make sure my tenants treat each other with respect?**

Living in multi-family properties can be challenging for some people. They may not be used to living in close proximity with others, and this can cause conflict. Some savvy landlords provide a written code of conduct with the lease, and they have tenants sign a form stating they have received a copy of it. The code should outline what is expected from the tenants, such as quiet hours, when and where they can use their grills, and where they can park. It's another simple form that will save you many headaches.

239. **One of the downsides of being an investor is that I have to deal with attorneys. I don't trust them. Is there any way to invest and live a lawyer-free life?**

I understand where you are coming from. I don't like dealing with attorneys, either. And I wouldn't trust them any further than I could throw them. They seem to make everything more complicated than it needs to be, and they are expensive.

But you have to deal with them if you make your living as a real estate investor. There is no way around it. You will need advice on how to draft leases, how to incorporate or establish an LLC, and you will eventually have to evict a tenant.

The best advice I can give you is to find an attorney you trust. She should make you feel comfortable, answer your questions without making you feel stupid for asking it, and return your calls in a timely manner. If you don't feel like your attorney is working for you, find another one.

You should also educate yourself. Some things, such as evictions, you can learn to do yourself until you can afford to hire a property manager. And that will save you tons of cash.

240. **Do I have to provide parking for my tenants?**

This varies from place to place. Some places require you to provide a spot for every person in the house who is old enough to have a driver's license. In other places, the amount of parking you need to provide will vary according to the square footage of the house. Educate yourself on what is required in your area.

241. **What color should I paint the interiors of my properties? I cannot decide between using all white to save time or adding a little color for a warmer feel. I have read that a little color can get units rented quicker and keep tenants longer. What are your thoughts?**

The main rule about painting interiors is that you don't want to go crazy in either direction. Paint the walls neutral colors, and you will match the furniture most people own. If you have purple or green walls you run the risk of chasing a lot of good tenants away. But if properties are all white, it may look clean enough to build microchips, and that's not good either. White walls with a few neutral accents works well.

Paint all your units the same colors. Being consistent will save you money and make your life easier. I use Sherman Williams for my paint. They can mix whatever color I need, and I don't worry about running out.

If you use the same colors in all of your properties, you won't have to carry around different buckets of paint wondering which paint goes in which unit. And if you allow tenants to paint the walls, make sure they paint them back or pay you to have it done.

242. **My new rental property doesn't have insulation. What should I do?**

You must have put on your thinking cap. You are asking difficult questions. I don't know of any states that require rental properties to be insulated, but be sure to check the rules in your area.

If not, it comes down to crunching the numbers. How much will it cost? If you pay to have it done, will it keep you from cash flowing? Is it a serious problem? If the property is in Northern Michigan it may be more serious than if it is in South Florida. Is it a big enough issue that tenants might leave if the heating bills are too much or the property stays cold? Insulation might be considered a capital improvement and not an expense, so there might be tax implications. I wouldn't install insulation unless the numbers were so good I had to.

243. **What is a joint venture?**

A joint venture is when investors come together for a specific property. It differs from a partnership, which implies that the investors have an ongoing relationship that will extend beyond one property or investment.

Joint ventures can be a great way to partner with someone and capitalize on their experience, knowledge, and money. But it won't tie you up forever. If the venture works, you can agree to do more deals in the future. If not, you go your separate ways when the project is done.

244. **Should I be an active or passive investor? Can I switch?**

I am an active investor. So active some people might think I am a caveman. Every day I grab my club, seek out the best deal I can, knock it over the head, and drag it back to the cave. That suits me well when the cycle is low and I can buy properties for bargain prices. But it can hurt me when the cycle is in a high stage. I have to turn the switch off and wait for the right time to buy.

You should be an active investor when the time is right. When prices are low and acquiring new properties helps build your portfolio. When you have financing in line and it makes sense. But you should be more passive when prices are high and when buying new properties kills your cash flow.

245. **Should I invest for income, capital appreciation, personal use, or a combination of those?**

Never consider your home or personal dwelling an investment. It is many important things, such as where you raise your children and where you dream about your empire. But it is not an investment.

Your investments should be focused on income and capital appreciation. Income helps you now. It puts food on the table, clothes on your back, and makes sure your children are safe. Capital appreciation helps you in the future. It gives you tangible assets that increase in value over the years. When the time is right you can sell them (if you want to) and have a big stack of cash to stuff in your bank account.

246. **What is an REIT?**

A real estate investment trust (REIT) is similar to a mutual fund for real estate investors. Investors can buy shares of stock of a REIT and enjoy the high returns that come from lending to real estate investors or investing in properties. There are several types of REITs, including equity REITs (which focus on owning properties) and mortgage REITs (which focus on loaning money to investors).

247. **Should I modify my current mortgage?**

Only if you crunch the numbers and it makes financial sense. If your lender is offering you a lower interest rate or you are able to borrow more money to buy more properties, a modification could be a savvy decision. Always account for the costs and fees associated with modifying any loan. You don't want to sign a deal and then realize your numbers are off because you didn't understand how much the modification was going to cost. You should never modify the loan for the sake of just doing it. It has to help you achieve your goals, help you grow your portfolio, and help you get to where you need to be.

248. Can I buy rental property after I file bankruptcy?

Yes. Everyone faces challenges in life, and sometimes that means financial difficulties that force people to file for bankruptcy protection. Once a bankruptcy is filed, there is a period of time (at least several months), where the bankruptcy is working its way through the system. There will be a hearing where the debtor (the person who filed bankruptcy) has to appear before his creditors (the people and companies who allege the debtor owes them money). The judge or magistrate may order the debtor to surrender the property to the creditors. After the hearing, the bankruptcy will be discharged or closed.

Once the bankruptcy is closed, you can borrow money and start buying properties. But there will be consequences. Bankruptcies will stay on your credit report for years, and no lender likes to see a borrower who has recently filed for bankruptcy. You may have to pay a higher interest rate or put down a larger down payment, but you can secure financing.

249. Help! Several of my units are empty. My cash flow is barely paying the bills, and the only people who have shown any interest in renting from me didn't pass my screening. Should I rent to them just to have rent coming in?

No. Stick to your guns, and don't make decisions when you are desperate. Renting to the wrong people is no way to get out of a temporary crunch. When you have challenges like this, get out and make things happen. Is your marketing plan as aggressive as it could be? Are your rents competitive for the neighborhood, or have you priced yourself out of the market?

And once things turn around, build an emergency fund so that you don't feel so much pressure the next time your business goes through a slump.

250. **What is a bird dog?**

This is not a four-legged friend who helps you hunt quail. A bird dog is someone who wants to help you make money and build your empire. Bird dogs are people who look for great investment properties. They may not have the resources or interest in buying and rehabbing properties, but they know investors who are always looking for deals. When a bird dog sees a potential investment property, he calls an investor and tells him about it. If the investor buys the property, he pays the bird dog a small finder's fee, ranging from a few hundred dollars to $500.

251. **How do I avoid being audited by the IRS?**

If you find a rock-solid, bulletproof answer to this question please let me know. We can patent the process and sell it to other investors. We will be buying yachts and Caribbean islands in a few weeks.

The best answer I can give is to follow the advice your accountant gives you. If he is experienced, he will know how to prepare your returns and make sure everything is properly prepared before you file your taxes. Make sure that he is willing and capable of representing you before the IRS in the event you are audited.

Always handle your business matters using the highest and best practices. Leave a paper trail as wide and long as you can, and don't take shortcuts. Avoid doing "under the table deals," because if a trained accountant starts going through your financial documents and the numbers don't add up, you will pay a steep price. It's not worth the risk.

252. **What is a Series LLC?**

A Series LLC is a special type of LLC that allows the creation of unlimited entities, or series, that act like individual LLCs. Each series has its own bank account, name, and may have different officers and directors. The advantage to investors is that it allows them to separate risks and provide legal protection without having to create a new organization. It makes the process of owning multiple LLCs cheaper and simpler.

Only a few states have authorized Series LLCs. You will need to check with your attorney to make sure they are available in your area and that one would be the right business structure for you.

253. What are HUD properties, and where can I find a list of them?

A HUD property is a property that was financed by an FHA Loan but was foreclosed. HUD homes can be bargains for investors, but you have to understand how the homes are sold. You have to go through a Realtor registered with HUD, and you should ask for an agent's NAID number before you make any bids on a property. If the agent can't provide the number, don't waste any more time with him. HUD has strict guidelines for how far it can deviate from its asking prices on properties, and those vary by region. If your offer is too low, it will automatically be rejected. Make sure your agent understand this process and can explain it to you.

You can find HUD properties at www.HUDhomestore.com. That site also has a list of all registered agents, and you can find the right one for you.

254. Can I assume a loan? If so, how do I do that?

An assumable loan is one in which the owner of a property can transfer title to a new buyer, and the buyer accepts the terms of the existing mortgage. Assumable mortgages can make it easier to sell properties, but not all loans are assumable. FHA and VA loans generally come with assignability clauses, but it may be hard to find other lenders who offer this.

The main advantage to buyers is that they receive the same interest rate the seller negotiated. If interest rates are on the rise, it's possible they may get a great rate. But, at the time I am writing this book, interest rates have been falling. Not many people are assuming loans. It is cheaper to purchase with a new loan at a lower interest rate.

255. My great handyman has had some rough times and needs a place to stay. Should I let him stay in one of my rentals in exchange for his services?

I am all for helping a brother out! I believe that when you become financially successful you have an obligation to help others in a responsible manner. I also believe in running my business like a business. And that means renting my properties out to people who pay me with green paper I can take to the bank.

Letting people use properties in exchange for services can be a nightmare if things go wrong. What happens if his work becomes shoddy? What if he gets sick and can't work? And if you have to let him go, can you just fire him or do you have to evict him as well? Don't mix business with the desire to help out a friend. Your business and your friendship may suffer.

Trust me on this one. I have taken it on the chin for more than $10,000 because I was trying to be a nice guy instead of a businessman. Don't let that happen to you.

256. How do I pull a potential tenant's credit report? What do I look for?

Looking at a person's credit report is a serious matter. You need her written permission to do it, and your application should include a clause that authorizes you to run a credit check. You will need the tenant's full legal name, date of birth, Social Security number, her employer's address, and her home address for the last two years.

You can submit a request for a report to one of the three major reporting agencies. They charge a nominal fee ($15 or less), and you should charge the prospective tenant the fee. Don't pay those fees out of pocket. It will eat into your bottom line.

Look at her credit score. What you want to see is someone who has a long history of responsibly managing credit. How long has she had her current credit cards? How much of her available credit has she used? Are there any unpaid accounts? Has she ever had debt written off as uncollectable?

You may have to read a few reports before they start to make sense. It will be worth your time, as reviewing someone's credit is the best way to determine if she will be responsible with her money and pay you on time.

257. I hired a crew to repair my house. The crew leader told me he wants me to purchase all the supplies and bring them to the job site. Is this typical? Will I have to do this every time I hire someone to work on one of my properties?

This is not typical, and it is not a good sign. Reputable, established companies will have credit accounts with suppliers, or they will be able to purchase supplies before the job begins. Most supplies should be included in the cost of the job. If you hire a painter, there should not be a surcharge for brushes. However, if you are using special order paint, that's a different story. But the contractor should supply the materials and bill you if needed.

258. The previous tenants in one of my properties were cat people, and the smell in the house proves it. One of the bedrooms is a converted garage. There was carpet over the concrete floor, but the carpet was soaked with cat pee. The carpet in the house was also used as a litter box. After I remove the carpet from these two areas, what should I replace it with?

I prefer Allure vinyl planks from Home Depot. If you crunch the numbers, it is cheaper to install and gives the most value over the years. You can install wood floors over concrete slabs, but you have to be certain that the concrete is dry. If there is excessive moisture, the wood will expand and contract. You should also consider installing a vapor barrier, especially if the property is in an area that is prone to moisture. You should also install a subfloor. Never install wood over new concrete. It should be at least thirty days old before you cover it with wood. Of course, wood floors can be installed inside a house with little or no trouble.

259. I just closed my first deal. When should I have the utilities turned on?

Never. Getting the utilities turned on is the tenant's responsibility. Do not hand over the keys until you are certain the tenant can have the utilities turned on in his name. A bad apple will occasionally get past your screening process, and having the utilities transferred over is one last test.

If the utilities are in your name, don't hand the keys over until the tenant has them transferred into his. If you turn them on and the tenant moves in without transferring them over, you may be stuck paying his bills. Use a checklist so that you don't forget.

260. If I don't turn on the water at one of my properties can the maids clean the house properly? Maids?

Must be nice to have the keys to the bank. Make sure your properties are as clean as possible when you show them to prospective tenants. A few dust balls or a shower that needs to be scrubbed can be the difference between a property that sits empty and one that cash flows. Maids (or a cleaning crew for the rest of us) will make a huge impact on how your properties look and how easily they rent. Make the maids' job easy. Keep the water turned on. Leaving the water on doesn't cost much if no one is living in the property, and that will yield dividends in the long run. But turn the water off at the meter when possible. You won't have to worry about leaks or broken pipes.

261. The gutters at one of my properties are full of leaves, and a tree branch has grown through them. Should I clean the gutters or replace them?

How did they get so bad? Why did you not see this during your regular inspection of the property? When was the last time you went and looked at the exterior of the property?

Problems like this are easy to avoid. By being proactive, you can save yourself time and money. You could have avoided this problem by simply looking at the gutters once or twice a year. I would do the cheaper option. Tenants won't care about gutters. None of them will crawl up on the roof and make sure there are no leaves in the gutters. The purpose of gutters is to protect your investment from water, and you should choose the option that fixes the problem with the least amount of money out of your pocket.

262. My newest property does not have central heat and air, but most of the houses in the area do. Should I install a new central heat and air system to make my property more marketable?

No. You will go broke trying to keep up with the Joneses. You will never build an empire if you base your financial decisions on what other property owners in the area are doing.

The only time you should install central heat and air is if the numbers add up. Heat and air is such a huge expense you will not recoup your investment for years, if not decades. I've done tons of deals, and I don't know of one that would justify the cost of a central heat and air system. Keep the money in your pocket.

263. Half the window blinds in my house are destroyed. Do I replace them or let the next tenant take care of the problem?

Before I answer that, how did they get damaged? Did the previous tenant do it, or did a bobcat sneak in during the night and tear things up?

If it was the previous tenant, make sure you deduct the amount from his security deposit. You are out of luck if the bobcat did it.

The blinds have to come down or be replaced. You don't want a prospective tenant to see them and think you don't care about your properties. It won't cost much to replace them and will help you keep rent-paying tenants in the property.

264. When doing a rehab, what's the best way to haul the trash to the big dump?

The last time I rehabbed a property, I put a dumpster out front and the neighbors filled it will their trash. When I have a big rehab or need to clean junk out of a property, I put an ad on craigslist. I find workers who are eager to work. They go through the property, clean everything out, and haul it to the dump. I don't have to worry about renting a dumpster or paying to haul away the neighbors' trash.

265. I'm not sure what the ARV will be on a prospective property. Should I call for an appraisal or pull comps off of the county website?

Being a savvy investor means watching your cash flow, and that means not spending one penny more than you have to. When you begin your investing career, you won't have a good sense of property values or reasonable prices to pay for investment properties. It may be money well spent to hire an appraiser. But after you have been in the game for a while, you won't need appraisers. If you have multiple properties in one area, you will know what houses sell for in the neighborhood. And you will know how to look up comps on your computer or smartphone and won't have to pay appraisers. To begin your search, point your browser to findcompsnow.com and eppraisal.com.

266. **Will a bank require a property to be insured for the full replacement value of the unit or will they accept something less?**

When your bank loaned you money, it was making an investment in you. After it looked at your credit history and the health of your company, it determined that you were a good risk. When they signed the check, it was a vote of confidence that you would pay the loan back as agreed.

The bank trusted you, but bankers are not stupid. They want to protect their investment, and that means you will be required to carry enough insurance on the policy to cover the full value of the property in the event you kick the bucket.

Of course, you should do everything you can to avoid dying before your loans are paid in full. The bank would be grateful, and so would your family.

267. **What are the early signs that a crappy neighborhood is turning into a good neighborhood?**

Finding properties in areas that are rough around the edges is a great way to build your portfolio. You can find diamonds in the rough and pay pennies on the dollar.

But you want the area to improve over time. That will increase the value of your properties and help you find better tenants. If you see homes that have great potential in an area that is less than desirable, drive through it every few months. Maybe the cars that were on blocks in front of the house at the end of the street have been moved. Hopefully, the dilapidated property in the middle of the block has been repaired or torn down.

But the best evidence that an area is turning around is to see another investor has taken a leap of faith and is putting money onto the area. If you see a house being painted, having a new roof installed, or getting new windows keep your eyes open. If you see a "For Rent" sign out in the front yard, it's time to buy. All it takes is one investor to turn around an entire neighborhood. One investor can be the spark that transforms an entire area. Investors want to protect their properties, and they will do what they can to get rid of homeowners who don't care about the condition of their houses or the people who live in them. Other investors buying property in a rough area are your allies. They will work for the same goals that you have. And the two of you can work miracles and provide safe housing for decent families and make ton of cash in the process.

268. **Should I have enough life insurance to pay off all of my mortgages if I die? This depends on your circumstances.**

Do you have a spouse or young children to support? Are they dependent on your investment income? If you die, who would take over the company? Would they be better off if you left them a lump sum of cash that could be invested or set aside for their futures? Or are you single with no dependents?

If that's the case, life insurance may be a waste of money.

Visit with your insurance agent and your attorney to make sure your estate planning, including insurance needs, are covered. Do it as soon as you can. Things can change in a heartbeat, and you want to do all you can to provide for your loved ones in the event something happens to you.

I carry enough life insurance to pay off all of my mortgages in the event something happens to me. My family will be able to pay off my houses and rely on the income from the rent. The peace of mind is worth every penny.

269. **A wholesaler called me about a house that he has under contract. Is it kosher to ask him the amount of his offer?**

You can ask, but no seasoned wholesaler will answer you. If he does, he is either a rookie who doesn't know how the business works, or he is playing you by upping the numbers. Wholesalers get properties under contract and then offer to sell the property for more money than they paid for it. There is nothing wrong with that, but savvy investors know wholesalers aren't likely to give up their secrets.

But it never hurts to ask, and the wholesaler might surprise you. He might tell you what he paid and what he thinks is a fair profit. Asking him could help you do one of the quickest deals of your career.

270. **What is a more effective way of finding good deals: using a good wholesaler or craigslist?**

There is no best way to find good deals. They are all the same. You have to get off your couch, get your ear to the ground and hustle. Part of the process of building your empire should include talking to wholesalers, scouring craigslist and placing ads in it, and using bandit signs. You should also drive through the neighborhoods where you want to invest and find properties for sale. Talk to your banker and to other investors.

The only bad ways to find properties are the ones you don't use. When you do nothing, other investors are buying houses and getting rich off of your laziness.

Get busy. If you don't, your life will never change. And you don't want to be in the same place five years from now, do you?

271. **I am looking for homeowners who have substantial equity in their homes. How do I find them?**

This will be a guessing game. You won't find a list that details how much equity people have, but you can find enough information that will give you the ability to make an educated guess. If you are interested in a certain neighborhood, you can pull up the property records of the houses in the area. You will be able to tell when the current owners purchased the houses and if there is a mortgage on the property. You may be able to tell how much the owners paid for the property by looking at the tax stamps that were issued at the time of purchase. With that information and the date of purchase you can estimate how much equity is in the property.

If you get lucky, there will a mortgage or lien release and you will know the property is owned free and clear. A savvy investor like you shouldn't have any trouble discovering the value of the property, which is all equity.

272. **I want to look up someone's mortgage. Can I do that? Okay, I'll bite. Why do you want to know the details of someone's mortgage?**

That question makes me wonder if you are a stalker.

Before I researched the answer to this question, I assumed that mortgages were private and that banks would not be able to release that information. But then I fired up my computer, typed a few words into a search bar, and instantly found sites that displayed mortgages. One of my mortgages was even posted on the site. It was an eye-opener and shocked me. We live in a digital age, where almost everything is available on the Internet.

Knowing the balance on a mortgage can be great information to have during a negotiation. It will give you an idea of a seller's bottom line. If that is more than you are willing to pay, you can pass on the deal before you waste any time.

If you want to try and track down someone's mortgage, start with your local county clerk's website. You will be amazed at what you will find.

273. I am a lady investor. I don't feel comfortable being alone with prospective tenants when I show them property. How should I handle this?

Thank you for asking this question. As a male investor, it's easy to forget that women investors unfortunately have to deal with circumstances that never cross my mind. You need to be as safe as you can when you are meeting with strangers in empty properties.

Your first meeting with a prospective tenant shouldn't be at a property. Have him meet at your office, and scan his driver's license or ID into your computer. If you are old school, make a photocopy. An even better way would be to prequalify the prospect. It's a waste of everyone's time if the tenant can't pass your screening process, and you might tell him he has to fill out a brief information sheet before you will show a property. You'll get his identifying information and can quickly check his criminal record online.

The most important thing to do is to trust your gut. Your instincts are some of your most valuable tools. Trust your inner voice. If something doesn't feel right, it's probably best to let him rent from someone else.

Another option is to hire someone to show the properties for you. I hired a college kid to show mine and he does a great job. He also keeps the outside of the property clean for a little extra cash. It frees me up to work on putting deals together.

274. I hired a crew to repair one of my houses. The crew leader told me before they started he needed me to bring them all the supplies. Is this normal?

No. This is a giant red flag, and you may want to think twice about using this contractor. Basic supplies such as paint and tape should be included in the negotiated price. Any contractor who has been in business for any time at all will have more tape than he can use, and he will have paint on hand or can buy it on credit at the local paint store.

Unless the paint is unusual or unique. If that's the case, he may want you to order and purchase it so that there is no confusion.

If you get a call from a contractor asking you to bring supplies to a job, don't be tempted to do it. You are an investor, not a delivery person. Your time is valuable, and you need to treat it that way. Will buying tape and paint make you wealthy? Would your time be better spent finding deals and buying properties? Think about it.

275. I want to get rich NOW. Should I quit my day job today and focus on investing in real estate full-time?

We all want to make stacks of cash. That's why you are reading this book, attending seminars, and looking at every property you come across. It's what you dream about at night and the thought that consumes you all day.

But you have to build your empire the right way. You need to start slow, with one or two properties. It will take time to build your cash flow to the point that your properties will support you and your family. In the meantime, you will have bills to pay and will have to buy food and clothes. I assume you are working because you need the money. Why else would you show up every day? Don't make the mistake of thinking investing in real estate is going to replace your current income before your next payday. Savvy investing will create a lifestyle you never dreamed of. But it takes time to do it right, and you need to keep the lights turned on in the mean time.

276. Do you ever recommend selling properties?

Yes. Selling properties can be a great way to build your portfolio. But it has to be the right property at the right time for the right price. You shouldn't sell any property just because someone makes you an offer. The sale has to be done as part of an overall investing strategy, and there are a few questions you have to ask. How will I replace the cash flow this property generates? Is the offer fair? What am I going to do with the money? How will selling this property help build my empire? If you don't have solid answers to these questions, don't sell.

The only exception would be if someone made a ridiculously high offer on one of my houses. The kind of offer that no sane, sober, and informed investor would make. Like three times the value of the property. If that happens, I will sign the deed as fast as the check clears the bank. I won't think twice, and neither should you. The market can fluctuate as much as 15 percent, and I have sold as much as 20 percent above retail.

277. Should I be concerned if I have a large amount of vacancies? Concerned? Yes, that might concern me. How can you ask that with a straight face?

You must enjoy flirting with bankruptcy, or maybe you like the prospect of living in a van down by the river. If your vacancy rate is too high, you will go broke. It's that simple.

If you have a hard time finding good tenants for your properties, you need to look at every aspect of your business plan. How are you marketing your houses? Do people know you have properties for rent? Are there problems with your properties? Do people look at your houses and hate the thought of living in those dumps? Maybe your rents are too high for the area. Have you become complacent about building your business?

Your vacancy rate is a reflection of the health of your company. If you ignore a low rate too long, your company will have to be admitted to the emergency room. And if that doesn't work, it will be fitted for a toe tag. Don't let that happen. Take care of problems as they arise.

278. Should I owner-occupy a property before I make it a rental?

This is not the best way to build an empire. The point of buying investment property is to build positive cash flow. You need tenants in your units, and you need them paying their rent on time each and every month. If you occupy a property, you won't get any cash flow. And that defeats the purpose of buying the property in the first place.

The only possible exception would be a duplex. Buying a duplex can be a great way to start your business. You live in one side of the property, and the rent you collect from the tenant living on the other side pays the mortgage. As you buy more properties, your cash flow should improve to the point that you can buy a home, move out of the duplex, and find a tenant to pay you rent.

279. Should I buy another property while I am rehabbing another?

The answer to this question will change as you grow your business. When you begin your investing career, buying another property while you are rehabbing can be a risky proposition. It's not unusual for things to go wrong during a rehab. Contractors may not finish on time, or once they start working they may find problems they didn't expect. If that happens and you buy another property, you will be paying holding costs and mortgages on two properties. And you won't be able to rent either one until the rehabs are done. It will put a strain on your cash flow. My advice is that you should start slow and wait until your first property is rented and making money before you buy a second.

Once you have a few properties, you can absorb the delay of a rehab. Then it won't be such a problem if one house can't be rented for a month or so.

Take it slow and do it right. Don't rush to buy your second property.

280. Is it savvy to pay cash for a property?

No. The savvy way to buy property is to use other people's money. If you leverage your cash, you may be able to buy three or four properties instead of one. You should never have more cash tied up in a deal than you absolutely have to.

Manage your debt carefully, and you will be able to buy more properties faster than you could by using your cash. And you will have additional deductions you can use when tax season rolls around.

281. Could you recommend a good get rich quick book or seminar for me?

Yes. The first title is Take My Money, Please by I.M. Stewpyd. The second book you should read is It Takes Work, Dummy by U.R. Dreemyn.

There is no way to get rich quick. People will sell you books and seminars that tell you it only takes a few minutes a day to build wealth, but the truth is that you will get out of your business what you put into it. If you work hard, stick to your plan, and stay focused, you can build an empire that will generate wealth for the rest of your life. If you want to take the easy way out and do things quickly, you won't get anywhere.

282. Can I pull equity out of rental my properties?

The only two ways to benefit from the equity in your properties is to sell them and put the cash in your pockets or borrow against them. Equity is a funny thing. It only exists on paper until you convert it to cash. And that means saying goodbye to the property or taking out another mortgage.

283. A prospective tenant came in and told me such a sad story I wanted to cry. He seems like a nice guy who is having a hard time. He didn't pass my screening process. Should I rent to him anyway?

When you own rental properties, you will hear a lot of tearjerkers. Some of them will even be true.

I am all for charity, but that ends at the front door to my office. I have to run my company like a business. If I don't, I won't be able to pay my bills, and my family and I will be the ones looking for handout.

If you want to help people in need, donate to a local charity. You can also keep a list of organizations that help people who need housing. But don't run your business like a charity. It will ruin you.

284. Is lease to purchase a good way to make money?

Lease to purchase can be a goldmine. Lease to purchase is a sales agreement. The buyer gives you a big down payment, pays you every month, but he doesn't own the property until it is paid in full. If he misses any payments, you can keep the property and all the money you have been paid. Some properties will be sold multiple times, and this means serious cash flow to the investor.

285. How much cash flow should I be making after a year or so?

I hope you make tons of cash from the first day you start investing. But it takes time to be a successful investor. There is a learning curve, and you will suffer a few bumps and bruises along the way. Your first year may be tough, and don't take that as a statement on your ability as a landlord. If you work hard and apply the lessons in the Savvy Landlord books, you can build an empire.

Where you will be at the end of your first year depends on how hard you work, how aggressive you are, and how much you learn. Think long-term about your investment properties. If you do things right the first year, you will lay the foundation for things to come, even if you don't see results right away.

286. I found a bargain property in a rough part of town. I rehabbed it but can't seem to attract the quality tenants I want. What should I do?

Bargain properties are usually bargains for a reason, including being in an undesirable part of town. Location is one of the most important factors for attracting decent tenants, and if you buy in the wrong part of town it will be challenging to find the right tenants. Regardless of how much paint you put on it, no one wants to live in the worst part of town. Sometimes, bargains aren't bargains. A few tips that might help are lowering the rent, taking the deposit over time, or, as a last resort, selling the property to a rookie investor.

287. What should I look for in a property manager?

There is no substitute for experience. Look for someone with a track record of working with investors on multiple properties. You don't want be the guy who pays for someone to learn the ropes. Choose your property managers carefully, and you can sleep at night. Ask other investors what companies they use. Hopefully you will hear the same name mentioned more than once. At the least, they should tell you the name of a company they would recommend.

It's also important to discuss work styles and expectations. The best manager in the world won't do you any good if you aren't on the same page in terms of communication styles. Some people like to text, e-mail, or video conference. Others like phone calls and faxes. Make sure that you and your manager understand when and how you will communicate. You don't want to think everything is fine because you haven't received any bad news via fax when your manager has sent you twenty e-mails about the fire that burned down one of your best properties.

And make sure your temperaments are suited for each other. Some people just don't click. There is nothing wrong with that. It doesn't reflect on either one of you, but you don't want to be in a situation where you don't get along with your manager. Don't be in a rush when you hire someone. Do your homework, hire the right person for the job, and let them take care of the daily grind of dealing with tenants. Don't you feel better already?

288. I am thinking about refinancing my mortgages. Should I do that when the rates are high or low?

Low. You want as little cash going out each month as possible, and this means negotiating the lowest interest rate possible on each and every mortgage. You can start by watching interest rates and understanding if they are rising or falling. Visit with your banker about where rates are going. If you time your refinance right, you can save a ton of cash just by waiting for them to fall. It's like making money for doing nothing. Doesn't that sound great?

289. Who is responsible for replacing the air filters in the HVAC system?

Savvy landlords take care of this themselves. It's the only way to make sure filters are changed on time. You should have a contract with a local HVAC company that services our units and handles this.

I have tenants sign a notice that states if the cause of a repair was an air filter that wasn't changed they will be billed $125 for the service call. If you wait for tenants to change filters, you will be buying a lot of air conditioners.

290. One of my tenants requested a doorbell. Do I have to install one?

No. Some tenants will ask for the moon. They will want covered parking, walk-in cedar closets, and twenty-four hour concierge service. If you installed everything your tenants ask for, you would go broke.

Your obligation as a landlord is to provide safe housing for a reasonable price. Anything beyond that will cost you money you don't have to spend. Keep the cash in your pocket.

291. How do I learn the value of a multi-family property?

Learning the value of multi-family property is no different than learning the value of a single-family property. The key is to gather as much information as possible. You can't make an informed decision about whether to buy or sell a property if you don't know what it is worth. You need the right information to determine the Net Operating Income (NOI) and cap rate.

Start by looking at other similar properties in the area. Have any of them sold recently? Can you look at the property records and estimate what the last selling price was? Talk to investors in your REIA club. Do any of them handle multi-family properties?

Visit with one of your real estate agent contacts. Has she handled any recent sales of multi-family properties? It's worth the cost of a lunch to find out and to get her input. And don't forget to talk to your lenders. If your banker works with many investors, he will have a good idea of the values of multi-family properties in your area. He won't be able to give you the specifics of any deals he has worked on, but at the least he might be able to introduce you to other investors. It never hurts to ask.

292. One of my tenants invited me to a party he is hosting this weekend. Should I go?

Keep your relationship strictly professional. When you are a landlord, you may have to make difficult decisions. The tenant who invited you to a party last month may be the deadbeat you have to evict next month. Don't let friendship cloud your judgment. Be polite and respectful, but trying to be friends with your tenants is a mistake.

293. **The lady who rents one of my properties has been a great tenant for eight years. She has never been late on her rent, and she keeps the interior sparkling clean. I just found out her disabled son has been living with her for eight weeks. Can I evict her?**

Why in the world would you want to evict a tenant like that? Technically, she may be in violation of her lease because she had someone else living in the property without your knowledge or consent. Technically, you might have the right to evict her. But is that the best decision to make? If you evict her, how long is it going to take to replace her? What if the next tenant has to be evicted three months later for not paying rent?

Compassion is underrated in the business world. Sometimes, doing the right thing is the best business decision. Talk with her about why your tenants can't have friends or family members sleeping on couches. You will keep a good tenant, and that is money in the bank. You may consider raising the rent by 10 percent to cover wear and tear.

294. **Should I advertise the fact I am looking to buy houses?**

Yes. A good marketing plan is crucial to growing your business. Your marketing plan needs to focus on at least two areas. You need to let people know you have properties for rent. If no one knows you are in business, they won't rent from you. And that means you will be stuck with mortgages you can't afford to pay.

You also need to let people know you are buying properties. Your business won't grow if you don't add more houses when the time is right. Are you happy with how much money you are making as an investor? Has your company flat-lined? Do you not see any growth on the horizon?

The only way to take your company to the next level and build a real empire is to increase your cash flow. And that means buying more properties. You should be busting your butt looking for new properties, but by telling people that you are looking to buy you will leverage your time. Even if those people don't have any properties for sale, they might have friends or family who do. Let them be your unpaid employees and encourage them to beat the bushes for you.

295. What would be the best way to get the word out I am scouting for houses?

There is no wrong way to find new properties, but your efforts should be part of an organized and focused marketing campaign. Do direct mailing to the owners of potential properties, use bandit signs, and place ads in local newspapers and craigslist. The more advertising you do the better. The only wrong thing you can do is nothing. You can't build a great portfolio by sitting on your couch.

296. Should I find a real estate agent to work with?

Yes. You need to be friendly with as many real estate agents as you can. Agents will have access to the MLS, and that will give you more information. Information is power, and it will help you make savvy decisions. Realtors may also have pocket deals, and if you know and work with one you may get the first shot at those deals. And your agent will know other agents, who will know people who want to sell properties. Of course, your agent is in business and will expect a commission or finder's fee on any deals she brings your way. Make sure to factor that into your offers and when you crunch the numbers.

You may be tempted to leave the agent out of the deal or to haggle over a commission. This might insult the agent, and she may not want to work with you future deals. Treat her right, and it will make you money in the long run.

297. **Do I need a real estate agent to make an offer on a property or to sell a property I own?**

No. You can (and should) make offers and sell most of your properties without an agent, especially after you have done several deals. Agents can help you tremendously, but they come with a cost. If you use an agent on every deal, you can kiss 3 percent of your cash flow goodbye. The margins will be tight on most of the deals you will do, and you don't want to throw your money away. The numbers will never add up if you do that.

298. **Should I go to real estate school and get my license?**

There is no value for most investors to get a real estate license. If you are only buying and selling for yourself, you won't need it. You won't learn anything new, because once you do a few deals you will have a degree from the School of Hard Knocks.

Real estate licenses have downsides. To keep a license costs money and you may have to attend continuing education classes. That is time and money that could be spent on putting deals together. You would also be bound by a code of ethics, and you might have obligations to do or say things that you wouldn't have without the license.

It sounds good to say you have a real estate license, but it's not a savvy move. Keep your money in your pocket and spend your time on your business.

299. **Is buying a duplex a better investment than buying a single-family home?**

There is no way to answer this without knowing more about the deals. Depending on the circumstances, either one could be the best deal. It all comes down to cash flow. In some cases, the duplex will be a better deal. In other cases, the house will be the clear choice.

As an investor, you can't get caught up thinking that one type of property is always better than another. Great deals come in single-family units, multi-family units, and commercial properties. Your job is to know the market, negotiate the best deals possible, and maximize your cash flow every chance you get. You have to be savvy every minute of every day and make the best of every opportunity that comes your way.

300. My insurance agent wants to insure my rental property for the replacement cost, which is four times more than I what paid for it. The monthly premium is 25 percent of my cash flow. How can I save money on my insurance premiums but make sure my property is covered?

It seems like insurance agents always want to sell you the most expensive product. After all, they make their money on commission, and many of their bonuses are tied to the value of their total sales.

You don't need to pay for replacement value. A better deal is after-rehab value, which would pay the value of the property assuming all the repairs and rehabs had been done. The premiums will be substantially less, and you will still be protected in the event your property is damaged or destroyed. You might also consider raising your deductible to a higher amount, such as $2,500.

301. I'm rehabbing several houses, and when I am done I am hiring a property manager to manage all of my investments. Should I purchase and install items such as stoves or ovens, smoke detectors, and HVAC filters before I turn the properties over to the manager? Or should I let him handle those things and charge me for them?

The better value is to replace the major items before handing them over. The property manager may charge you for the time and expense of handling the rehab, and you don't want or need the additional cost when the properties can't generate income. Plus, handling the rehabs by yourself gives you control over the project. You can negotiate the best prices on any major items that need to be replaced.

But I wouldn't waste my time replacing small items, such as air filters. One of the benefits to hiring a property manager is that he handles the day-to-day operation of your empire. You won't have to think about light bulbs, air filters, or leaky toilets. Let the manager handle those issues, and you can worry about buying more properties and generating more cash flow.

302. I have to replace the HVAC system in one of my properties. Should I buy an expensive one that is less likely to break or the cheapest unit I can find?

You should always buy the best value. Cheap units will save you money at the start. You won't have to use as much cash to buy them, but the reality is that they may require more maintenance. More expensive units will require more money out of pocket, but they generally have a reputation as being more reliable and lasting longer.

This decision will become easier as you gain experience. You will develop a sense of the maintenance costs associated with HVAC systems and the relative value of expensive and cheap systems.

It's hard for me to justify spending money on an expensive system. There is no guarantee they will last longer or have fewer problems than cheaper ones. And I would rather pay my handyman or my HVAC contractor to fix a system than to pay for a new one. If you have to bite the bullet, make sure you are buying the unit from a contractor who will provide a written warranty and will service the unit.

TEN SAVVY TIPS

❶ **Require tenants to give you their middle names on your applications.** It is a small detail, but it makes a world of difference if you have to sic bill collectors or a process server on someone. Even if you only get a middle initial, it helps you sort out your deadbeat tenants from all the other people who share their names. It will also make it easier if one of your tenants has gone by her middle name in the past.

I learned this the hard way. One of my tenants didn't pay her rent, and I had to evict her. She didn't give me her middle name when she completed the applicati on, and when I checked her out online, she looked like a great tenant. But when I discovered her middle name and checked her out with that information, warning signs popped up all over the place. She had been evicted multiples times and wasn't the kind of person I wanted renting from me. Had I been firm about having her middle name, I never would have rented to her and would have saved myself a ton of headaches.

❷ **After you and a seller have reached an agreement on the price of a property, file a "Notice of Contract" with the county clerk.** I learned this tip a few weeks ago and wish I had learned it sooner. Buying real estate is a tough business. When money is involved, some people get greedy and throw their integrity out the window. Here's a scenario that has happened to almost every seasoned investor I know. You and a seller reach an agreement, but before you can get him to sign a contract another investor shows up and offers him more money than you did. The seller gets greedy and justifies his actions by saying he didn't have a contract with me, only an offer. You get screwed out of a sweet deal because not everyone honors his handshakes as much as you do.

I learned that you can go to the county clerk's office after you have an agreement to buy a property and file a "Notice of Contract." It puts the world on legal notice that you have a deal pending, and if the seller doesn't honor his commitment to you, the title to his property will be clouded. It's a simple document, but you need to include the address and legal description of the property. It's cheap insurance to protect the time and energy you put into making a deal happen.

❸ **If you live in an area where there is any chance of your pipes freezing, always winterize your vacant properties.** I speak from experience on this one. It's on the long list of things I have learned the hard way. Take these words to heart, and don't throw money out the window like I did.

Last winter, I owned sixteen vacant properties. Like a fool, I didn't take the time to winterize them. Nothing had happened to the properties before, and I assumed my properties would be safe. They weren't. Pipes froze and broke in every one of them, and I suffered more than $150,000 in damage. I spent a lot of time with insurance adjusters and paid a lot of money. I could have avoided the situation by picking up the phone and telling my handyman to winterize the property. Don't be a fool like I was. Be proactive.

❹ **Have tenants sign an "As Is" document when they move in.** This piece of paper will save you time and headaches. It simply states the tenant accepts the property with unnecessary repairs, such as torn screens. Some tenants will take advantage of your good nature and will call about every minor imperfection. You will spend nights and weekends discussing dings on appliances or scratches in bathtubs if you don't have an agreement. It's another simple way to make your life easier.

❺ **Investing in a $10,000 CD at a commercial bank can be a great way to find a new lender.** Banks like doing business with people they know. Giving a bank money to invest is a great way to start a new relationship. You will know some of the tellers and officers when it's time to fill out an application, and it will make it easier when you need a loan. It also makes you look like you are committed to the bank.

❻ **Two words: smell bombs.** These are my new best friends. I wish I had known about them years ago. After some tenants move out, you will be shocked what your property smells like, especially if they have pets.

One of houses smelled like cat pee when I entered the property to get it ready to rent. I went to the local home improvement store and discovered the magic of smell bombs. They look like bug bombs. You set the cans in the middle of each room, activate them, and they spray fog. But instead of killing bugs, they kill odors. You can purchase my favorite, Misty Alpine Mist Extreme-Duty Odor Neutralizer Fogger, at www.globalindustrial.com. Keep a few of these on hand for properties that get funky. You will thank me later.

❼ **The newest and best roach solution is Maxforce FC Magnum Pest Control Bait.** I love this stuff. You can get it at your local hardware store, and you don't need a license to use it. Your properties will attract bugs, and roaches are the worst. Use this stuff when you need to get rid of uninvited pests, especially roaches.

❽ **Resolve disputes early.** This is not just good advice for real estate investors. It is good advice for everyone. When you and a tenant don't see eye-to-eye, do what you can to take care of the situation. I am not saying you should be a doormat and give in to whatever crazy demand your tenant throws at you. But it is cheaper and less stressful to take care of small problems before they become big ones. You don't want to lose a tenant or to be sued when you could have solved the situation with a phone call or changing a few light bulbs.

⑨ Establish regular office hours, and stick to them. When you work for yourself, it is easy to allow your job to become your life. If you a regular nine-to-five job, you leave the office at the end of the day, and you can forget about your work until the next morning. But when you own a company, you may be tempted to pick up the phone every time it rings. Voicemail was created for a reason. If you don't give yourself a break from work at nights and on the weekends, you won't last long. You will burn out, and your relationships will suffer. Most things can wait until the morning. Even if your property is on fire, tenants should know enough to call 911. There is nothing you can do if they call you. If you went to the property and tried to help the fire department you would only be in the way. And watching your property burn would be heartbreaking. Spare yourself the pain.

⑩ Have reasonable expectations. If you build your business on the proper foundation, you can create an amazing lifestyle for you and your family. You can make a ton of cash and do things most people will never dream of. But it won't happen overnight, and it will take a lot of work. You will make mistakes, some of which will cost you money. You may get frustrated and wonder why you ever thought buying investment property was a good idea.

All of those things are part of the process. Investing can have a steep learning curve, and you probably won't make tons of cash when you first start out. But if you think and plan long-term, you can build something special.

INTERVIEWS

I am a big believer in learning from those who have gone before you. If you find someone who has built a profitable real estate investment portfolio and ask her the right questions, you can shave a lot of time off your learning curve. You can do in months what it would take others years to do. And you can avoid some of the costly, embarrassing, and frustrating mistakes most investors make.

That is why I have included interviews with other investors in the Savvy Landlord books. Study these questions and answers. Learn from the people who have done what you are trying to do.

JESSICA WATSON

I met Jessica in the most random way. I operated a booth at a local home and garden show and she picked up one of our free CDs. She listened to it and realized that if I could make a living as an investor so could she. Jessica is only thirty-one years old and has been investing for less than a year, but she already owns four properties. She is motivated to be financially free, and you can learn from the example she has set.

How did you hear about the Savvy Landlord?

I went to the Oklahoma City Home and Garden show. I was looking at stuff to possibly do with my house, and I just wanted to go for fun. People were handing out the CD bonus material from your first book. I thought your CD was probably a scam, but I put it in my bag, and didn't even look at it for three weeks. I listened to it and liked what I heard. I looked on your website, and I took a few classes. I enjoyed what I learned and signed up for mentoring.

Did you own any rental property before you received the CD?

No.

What made you decide to invest in real estate?

In college, I volunteered with Habitat for Humanity every week, and I learned a little bit about home buying and home construction and repairs in general. I thought it was interesting. When I graduated, I bought a condo for myself with the help of my grandparents, and I went through the buying and selling process with that. I bought a house for myself after I sold the condo, and I went through the buying process again. It was interesting to see different home values and how some houses could be fairly inexpensive, but if you knew how to fix them and do things that you could make them worth a good amount of money.

A friend's sister did some flips, and I watched her do those. I thought, "Yeah, I could do this. This could be fun." I read a few books. After I listened to your CD I decided buying and holding properties would be a better route to go. So I started moving that direction.

How would you rate yourself as an investor on a scale from 1 to 10?

About a 6.

What are your long-term goals? Where do you see yourself?

I want to buy seven more properties in 2015. I would like to own ten by the end of the year. That would provide enough income to cover all of my expenses and everything that I have. I would feel pretty comfortable with the amount that I could make off of that. As far as long term goals, I would like to make enough where I could be a stay-at-home parent and be more financially independent. That would free up time to travel, which is something I'm really passionate about. I won't have to worry about a schedule, because I'll be totally flexible with real estate.

I know you have an interesting story about financing. Would you share that with our readers?

Just because you have money doesn't mean the bank is going to be willing to loan you money. I had a family issue come up, and I'd ended up quitting my full-time job. I was working part time for a friend. I didn't really have a lot of debt. I had good credit. I had some money I had been saving.

My plan was instead of putting all the money into buying one house, I would divide that money up over several houses to build my business. It sounded like a great idea. I thought banks would look at me and say, "Here's a person who doesn't have a lot of debt. She doesn't have a lot of bills, and she has this money." All I was doing was asking them to let me borrow money against my money. But it turned out to be a little bit more difficult than that.

The first bank said that I would have to prove my real estate business was covering all of my bills in order to get a loan from them. I had to get out of the rat race in order for them to give me a loan. I owned two properties free and clear at the time. They were doing well.

But the loan officer said, "You need at least two or three more to totally cover your personal bills and everything, and then we could make a loan to you."

I said, "If I do that, I'll have no cash left to invest in anything." I wanted to grow it a lot bigger than four houses, and I would have been out of money at that point.

I hadn't been reckless, and I could document that I hadn't spent more than what the properties were bringing in. But it was something that we couldn't get around. So I ended up going to another banker, and it was super easy. There were no problems at all.

What was your goal with that loan?

I had two houses paid off, and one I wanted to pull the equity out of and divide it into down payments on multiple houses, or repairs if I needed to.

The loan officer owns rental properties, too. That helped because she understood what I was talking about. She understood where I was coming from. She basically said, "As long as you can show you have them rented, it's no problem, because you can show cash flow."

The loan included a balloon payment, but that's standard with her bank. She pretty much guaranteed me that as long as I paid it that there wasn't going to be any problem with the balloon and they would renew the loan.

Tell us about the first properties you bought.

The first was on HUDhomestore.com. It was listed like any other property on MLS. The other three were all on an online auction site.

I went to a few sheriff sales and other auctions, and the properties were all going back to the bank, which was frustrating. It takes a lot of research for me to be prepared, and then once I got there, most of the properties weren't sold. I was like, "Well, if it's going back to the bank, how are they selling it later on?" I found out that some of these properties were listed on MLS, but they sometimes ended up on different auction sites. I started checking different auction sites and searched under my zip code. All of the properties that were available popped up weeks in advance. It gave me lots of time. I could mosey on by the property or look up the information. It gave me a lot of time to research without worrying about putting in an offer immediately with somebody.

Sometimes the properties would have open doors or open windows. I could look inside and get a pretty good feel for the house.

I calculated out the repairs that I could see, and looked to see how much the house was going to be worth after I fixed it. Then I always calculated in extra money in case something went wrong. I tried to buy houses at 75 percent value. I'm not spending more than the house is worth. I'm still under what the house is actually worth. It might not turn out to be a great deal, but I could sell it as long as I wasn't underwater.

Do you have any tenant stories?

My tenants have been really great. They pretty much pay their rent on time, and I don't really hear anything from them. So that's been really nice. I drive by the properties, and they look great. One of my tenants even decorated the house for the holidays with really nice decorations.

I will say that I had a woman that I was going to put in a house. She seemed like she was on board. I did her credit check, her background check, her application. I held the house for her for a few days, because we were supposed to meet and sign a lease. I had a strange feeling, and I have learned to go with my gut. She ended up backing out, and I had to start all over again.

What advice would you give to a newbie or a female investor?

Educate yourself as much as you can. Join your local real estate groups and network with people. Get to know people. The best thing that happened to me was finding a mentor, because it saved me a lot of time and a lot of headache that would have frustrated me. You're going to have plenty of frustrations no matter what, but if you have people in your area or a mentor your life will be much easier. Even books and blogs can be really helpful and alleviate some of that stress.

I had a little bit of exposure to construction from my family and volunteering, so I know a little bit, and that helped. But there is definitely a stigma when you meet with a contractor, and they realize you are female. They speak to you differently.

I took a few classes, and I learned about things like homewyse.com, and some other sites where you can go on and get estimates for things that you need to have fixed. If you'll go on there and educate yourself a little bit about what's going on in your house, when you meet with that contractor and you have some knowledge, you can say, "It should be about this many square feet. I think it should cost this much, or it should cost that much." They realize that you're a knowledgeable person. It changes how they talk to you.

Are you where you want to be? What does the future hold for you?

I think everybody is always wanting to grow and move forward. I'm at the point where I'm going to start breaking even with the houses that I have and my personal expenses. Obviously, I want to exceed that so that I've got some extra money coming in.

I don't have a lot of debt. I'm fortunate in that I don't have a lot of expenses right now. But I'd like to be making more than I am. As I said, my goal for the year is to own ten properties.

Have you had an ah-ha moment?

The biggest realization I had was while I was working on my other house. I just said, you know, I've kind of been treating this as a fun game or a hobby, rather than a business, and that I really need to make some new goals for the next year to really ramp things up if I want to get it done quickly. I can trickle along and get 1 or 2 houses a year for a long time. But if I really want to achieve my goals, and be good to go by my mid-thirties I'm going to have to treat it a lot more like a business than I have been.

How do people respond when they know that you're in real estate, and you're only thirty?

Most people think it's exciting, but most people also really don't understand or appreciate even what it means, which is okay with me. When I'm dating someone they may say, "So you're a property manager?" I tell them, "Yep, pretty much." I don't say a whole lot about it. There are younger investors, but there aren't a ton of younger investors. Most of the people I date don't really have a good grasp of what it takes and what I'm really doing.

Are there any books you would recommend?

The Savvy Landlord was amazing. Not too long I listened to the goal-setting stuff by Jim Rohn, and that helped me think about what I really want to do.

Of course, Rich Dad, Poor Dad, but everybody says that that was like their great moment. It was enlightening for me just thinking about how my parents were raised and I was raised, and how I see other kids raised, and what you do and don't teach your kids. It's been interesting to compare. When I first told my dad I was going to do this, he wasn't unsupportive, but he was very hesitant about a lot of things. He asked, "Are you sure you want to do this? What kind of rent are you going to get? What kind of percentage is that? Is that better than the stock market? Is that better than working? What if you put this money in a Roth IRA?" He was very skeptical of how this was going to work out. But about a month ago he told me that he was really proud of me, and he was so happy it was working out well, and that I was doing well. That meant a lot to me. He said, "If I was younger, I think that's something I should have done more of." I told him, "You could do it now."

I've started reading Change Your Thinking, Change Your Life, and that's been really good for me, too. What stopped me in real estate was second guessing myself a lot and worrying about stuff, when really I never made a super risky choice or decision. So that book helped me think about what I'm doing.

AUGIE BYLLOTT

Augie is a rock star. This is one of the longest interviews I have pub-lished. He brings an incredible amount of wisdom and experience to the table, and leaving out some of the things he says would deny us a great opportunity to learn. When I interviewed him I had countless "Aha" moments and heard nugget after nugget. I could listen to him for hours and plan on attending one of his classes. He is encouraging, en-gaging, and genuine. He makes me want to be a "transaction engineer."

You're a school teacher now. Are you still investing in real estate?

We still have an active investing business. I do two kinds of investing. I do buy and hold, and I also do buy, fix, and sell. We're probably doing more fixing and flipping and we're maintaining and slowly growing our rental portfolio. What makes the decision as to whether we're go-ing to buy, fix, and sell or buy and hold is how we actually acquire the property. One of the things I teach my students is that the acquisition methodology will most likely dictate your exit strategy.

I believe in managing, running effectively, and money that's moving, money in motion, is usually growing. Money that's tied up is not neces-sarily growing. If I'm investing a lot of cash into a transaction, then it's likely going to be buy, fix, and sell. Whereas, if I'm buying on terms, which we do a lot of and it's a lot of what my students do, then if I'm not using a lot of capital. I'm getting tremendous leverage and I'd rath-er use the buy and hold kind of scenario.

When you say buying on terms, are you talking about creative financ-ing or general banking?

It's basically creative financing. Out of 400 transactions, I've only had two bank loans. I haven't used bank financing in seven or eight years, so it's what some people qualify as creative financing. I call it transac-tion engineering. The transaction works for all parties involved: buyers, sellers, and investors.

We do options. We do leasing, sandwich leasing. We also will buy property subject to an existing mortgage, and we have had no difficulty with taking over payments because we use a very specific process that makes sure we cross all the Ts and dot all the Is.

How many transactions have you done over the last eight years?

We have done 400 transactions in the last eight or ten years.

How did you come across real estate?

I was a banker for twenty-two years. In the early 1980s, the bank had major problems and they caused a lot of people to worry about losing their jobs. I was a new sales guy at the time. We had these guys who were national sales executives and they were the big guns. They would barely give little peons like me and my peers the time of day, except for one fella, Al.

When everybody else was running around worried about losing their jobs, Al was very cool, calm, and collected. One day I asked Al, "Why is it that you're the only guy in the entire office who is not stressed?"

He said, "I'm only going to work another two years."

I said, "Al, you're only forty. You're only going to be forty-two years old. What gives?"

He said, "I've been with the bank fifteen years and every year since I started I've bought one or two houses. I have these tenants who are paying off my houses. We've been making extra payments on a number of these houses so in the next two years almost all of them will be free and clear and the others will be almost paid off."

I started thinking to myself that this guy was working a regular job and he was buying these houses as a bank employee. It blew my mind that this guy at forty-two years old was able to say, "If I want to continue to work, I'll work. If I don't want to continue to work I'll stop, but either way I'll never have a problem paying my bills." This was back in the early 1980s, over thirty years ago. He had been investing in real estate since the early 1960s or 70s, so even if the houses were worth $70,000 or $80,000 that guy was going to be a real millionaire.

At the time I was probably making $20,000 a year. It took me a few years before I was able to buy my first house. I didn't do a lot of investing in the bank industry, but we did some, and that helped put me in a position where I could stop working twenty years later, at least in a corporate environment. When we moved to Florida, back in 2003, we ended up really getting into it. When we got to Florida I started to learn more about the creative side of real estate investing.

After I moved up the food chain in the banking industry, one of my bosses, a senior VP, and I were at lunch one day. He said, "I know everybody thinks I'm cheap." This guy would meet you for coffee and you would always have to pay. He said, "I never have a dollar in my pocket. It's all invested." He had a home on Long Island. He had another house in the Hamptons. He had one villa in Colorado and another one in Palm Beach, Florida. What I realized, again, this guy was using these for vacations but then he would rent them out and they would be high-end rentals in areas of extremely high demand. If he could rent them for four months out of the year he could cover his mortgage and taxes for the year.

When I calculated the value of what those were going to be worth by the time he had them paid off, he would be a multi-multi-millionaire because he'd probably have somewhere in the order of, in today's numbers, probably $15,000,000 worth of real estate.

These two guys were really great inspirations for me. Both of those men were willing to sacrifice in the short term for tremendous long term success, and they achieved it. I realized that as part of any wealth-building portfolio, you need one element at least that is very predictable. Real estate, if done properly, can be very predictable. I can't predict depreciation. I can't predict price fluctuations, but I can certainly predict cash flow.

If I have free and clear properties and some guy has invested in property next door but owes money on it, if the market rent comes down I have a lot more flexibility than he does. I like that you can invest safely and profitably and over the long term, anyone can get financial freedom.

But what I really like about real estate is the fact that it's the only business I know where the little guy is on a level playing field with big corporations.

When did you purchase your first house?

Back in 1983. I wasn't even sure it was an investment until I converted it from a single-family unit to a multi-family unit. I became a landlord and that cut my mortgage payments in half, which was a big deal because my first mortgage was at 14 percent with a bank loan. That wasn't hard money. That made a big difference. That house paid for itself.

That was the beginning. I left the corporate world back in 1999 or 2000. I had done well in my corporate life as well as in real estate investing. I was only an investor for three-and-a-half years, and I didn't draw a paycheck the entire time. But we lived just fine.

When we moved to Florida I thought I would continue in that venue, but I had a different plan. I thought I would buy a few houses, flip them after a year, and have some properties with some cash flow. I was also doing provincial ministry work, and one thing led to another. My real estate business got bigger, and we helped people avoid foreclosure and bankruptcy. A lot of times I wouldn't buy their houses. I would just give them counsel to help them see their financial picture from a different perspective. When they found a solution, they didn't have to leave or sell the house.

In some cases we did buy houses. We started to build a pretty healthy referral business. I feel really blessed with things they've gone the way they have. I never said we could teach. I'd like to say it's just this tremendous plan where everything just fell into place, but I believe in abundance and opportunity. If we are prepared when opportunity knocks and have our arms open ready to receive it, we're going to do really well. It's been more evolutionary, if you will, than revolutionary.

How long have you been teaching? When did you start PACT? (Parents and Children Together)

It's a funny story with the way it evolved because my intent was never to teach. I'm careful about saying stuff I'm definitely going to do because God may have other plans.

I came upon the idea in 2003 shortly after I went to a real estate sella-thon. One of these events where you've got ten speakers in the course of a day. Everybody gets ninety minutes and promotes whatever they are selling. I was fascinated by some of the content that I was reading about and learning about. We ended up spending a fair amount of money that day. I didn't know if my future would be in conventional investing, and it wasn't, but I always liked the idea of increased leverage.

One of the things the speakers said was you could join the local REIA and we did. We found Central Florida Reality Investing Association and my wife and I joined, and they were asking for volunteers. They asked me if I would host a focus group. I had no idea on what subject. They said, "Well, whatever you're doing is working. What are you doing?" I said, "I'm doing something called transaction engineering and it's a lot of different techniques." That's how the Investment Techniques Focus Group was born in the spring of 2004.

We had a great start. We had three to four people come to every meeting. It grew over time, and about a year and a half or so into our group being together, it grew to about twenty people, including a lot of new-bies. In one month, we'd get like $2,000,000 in transactions. I thought that was a pretty big deal so I wrote an article for our newsletter. The word got out, our attendance continued to grow, but at that time our executive director said to me, "Could you teach a seminar?" My first response was, "On what?" She said, "Well, obviously something's going on in the group. Some are learning, and doing, and taking action. They're buying houses and obviously making some money."

I did a seminar. I was shocked that people actually showed up and that was the beginning of our education business back in 2005. It went well enough that we felt there should be other ones. The first one was on lease options. The second one I did was on buying subject to organized strategies. Before I knew it I was teaching a number of different strategies. People started asking me, "Where can I get your information?" I said, "I just taught you everything I know."

We had no concept of recording any of this stuff but the question caused the information business to be born. About a year later, Realty Business was born. A few friends I had made in the business said, "You really need to do a coaching program." I said, "No, I don't because I don't have the time."

It turns out that I did have time, and I agreed to do one. Twelve people signed up for it, and by the middle of that six-month program we had a waiting list for another program. When we did the second one, I swore that there was an opportunity to reach a much broader base of clients, both buyers, sellers. It was helping other people to build new lives and careers.

Who inspired you?

People like Jack Miller. He was a great mentor and fan. Jimmy Napier is another guy that's been around for a long time. Pete Fortunato for a period of time. These are some of the names that come to mind. They're icons in the business of real estate, especially creative real estate, because the one thing that they bring to the table is a willingness. Maybe that's why they resonated with me, the idea that our primary objective is meeting the needs of other people.

If we can find a way to work with somebody similar then it's going to be good for her and good for us. If it's not going to be good for both parties I'm candidly not interested. There are a lot of win-win deals, and those are the ones I like.

That philosophy has been helpful for me because I don't have to do a lot of marketing to do a lot of business. The majority of our business is through referrals, through ventures, those kinds of things. We feel that we've built a good business.

I saw a lot of big-name platform pitchers selling really expensive programs to people who couldn't afford them. I watched unsuspecting people spend $30,000, $40,000 as much as $90,000 to get back nothing in return. It's the same kind of stage that says I can be your coach, and I can be your mentor. But they never tell folks, "What I'm really going to do is put you on the phone with somebody out in Utah and they're going to read from a computer screen. You may or may not learn something."

My belief is that you've got to work directly with people. I felt there ought to be an affordable alternative and that's what really led to the creation of our education training business. Because nobody should have to risk his life savings to test the waters.

What advice would you give someone who's just starting in real estate investing?

I have no issue with people getting bank loans if they know what their purpose is. I prefer you get private funds, private money because you can always deal with a human being. You can't deal as well with an institution. In today's day and age, if you can get cheap, fixed rate, long-term money that could be a good investment vehicle so long as you know what it is you're doing.

A lot of investors got tricked into lousy debt financing and they ended up with debt. They ended up with ten or twenty loans. These are not very healthy and can be quite toxic. With someone new, they have to learn some fundamental things.

First and foremost, what is their objective and how committed are they to it? Investing can be a tough business and it can be a great business but it's not an easy business. You have to know what your goals are and what you are willing to do to achieve them.

They also need to learn about creating and presenting offers. Our philosophy is we never give a person a single offer. We make multiple offers because there's more than one way to buy your property. Why should I dictate to you? It's like a lot of things, where you throw them against the wall and see if what sticks. I'd rather approach the prospect or the customer from the quantity. "Look Mr. Seller, there's a number of different ways I can buy your house and I'm going to share each one with you. One's going to be all cash, one's going to be some cash now and payments, and the highest offer is often going to be something that's going to be an installment package transaction where I will pay you the most money over a period of time. I can't presuppose to know what's best for you and your family, so I want you to choose one that makes the most sense for you."

That's a more collaborative approach to getting the transaction done. People have to learn how to create and present their offers. You've got to be able to handle objections and questions and feel good about it. We have to develop some skills that allow us to deal with those things.

Also, when somebody's new to the business, how do they intend to finance the transactions? Do they have access to capital? If not, how will they find money? Sometimes we access capital by simply creating it with the terms we use to deal with transactions. Over time you want to build relationships with private lenders. You want to be able to find good contractors. You need to learn how to manage tenants. A lot of people think, "Oh, man I want to buy rental properties. I want passive income." The IRS defines it as passive but you know as well as I do a good landlord is not a passive person. Property management is not a passive business.

You have to be actively engaged in the way you manage your tenants. Our host tenants are living in assets that are going to have a significant impact on our long-term financial well-being. We're giving our tenants keys to an investment that's worth $30,000, $40,000, $50,000, $100,000, or $200,000. It's no different than handing somebody a briefcase full of cash. Now granted that's a little bit more mobile than a house but they can destroy your house as quickly as they can and walk away with your briefcase with money.

You really want to learn how to manage tenants.

I think the first thing any new investor should do is invest ninety to 180 days in some kind of business planning, some kind of education so that they have an idea of what it is they're committing to. Our coaching program, PACT, stands for Personal Action Coaching and Training. That's the acronym, but it stands for four pillars that I really believe in: passion, action, commitment, and transformation. If you're new at investing it means you're not an investor today. You're not a landlord today. You have to become an investor. You have to become a landlord. That's a transformative process. You're changing from who you are to who you're going to become. Who you become is someone who creates more value than you create today. That's why we get compensated. We create more value today than we did yesterday so our compensation changes because our value has increased.

Tell me about your best deal.

I was approached by a wholesaler who had a contract on a fourplex. He came with a mortgage that I was able to subject to and he put a lot of money for renovations, about $80,000. What made it attractive was that each of the four units in this fourplex had their own property ID number or tax ID number, which meant I could buy it as a single investment but I could sell it piece meal. It was kind of like owning a bar, where you can buy a bottle of Scotch for about $8 and then sell it for about $1 a shot. Buy it by the quart and sell it by the shot is a seemingly great way to make money. It's great economic theory.

Here was the same thing in real estate. I could buy by the quart and sell it by the shot. We bought it with basically no money down. We were able to rehab it with no money out of our pocket because we got private money involved. We were able to sell it, but I didn't want to sell it quickly because the tax consequences would have been significant. We rented each of the four units for a period of time, and we also sold an option to each tenant buyer, which gave us enough time to seize on the property, qualify it as an investment rather than inventory. We qualified for long-term capital gains treatment and ended up with a six-figure paycheck when all was said and done. It only took fifteen months.

What was nice was when four new tenants starting moving in about four months into the project, they each paid $10,000 an option, which was like getting a zero interest loan because no taxes were due on that money until the options were exercised or they expired. It was a transaction that threw an additional $40,000 in usable cash in the middle of the transaction.

This is a transaction where we used a lot of the creative techniques I teach. We purchased the property in part by taking existing mortgage subject to. We had to give the wholesalers half of their wholesale fee and the other half they were willing to wait for. They got a very healthy figure, $60,000. You might ask, "Who would pay a $60,000 wholesale fee?" Somebody who was going to make three times that.

I didn't plan to make as much money as I made. It was a steal in the market and we finished the project on time and on budget. The property was near a local university and we found four parents who each wanted to buy a place for their kids. The kids lived in the property instead of a dorm.

It worked out beautifully, and to date I would say that's probably been the most fun transaction. We've had others that were fun but this one used a lot of techniques I teach. In addition to the money we took subject to, a private lender came into the deal and infused a substantial chunk of cash, and he didn't need any payments. He got paid off once the entire transaction was completed. We were able to use subject to and some seller financing because of the finance wholesale fee, and we also had the benefit of private money. That's three separate techniques. When we sold it we gave the buyers options, and as an incentive to the buyers we gave them a discount to the market if they would all close within a seven-day period. We told them they're going to get their $10,000 benefits but if they run a day late the price goes up $10,000.

They bought the equity, but we also did very well because the markets were improving, and we ended up making 20 percent more than we originally anticipated.

Can you share a story about something that went wrong?

Early in my investing career I had some money burning a hole in my pocket, and I was very frustrated because I was attending auctions regularly. I would always get outbid. One day I decided I was going to buy something if it was the last thing I did. The short version is that I didn't do enough research, and I bought a second mortgage unbeknownst to me.

I'm thinking I got this killer deal for $45,000. I thought the house was worth $120,000, maybe $130,000. I'm thinking I must be the smartest guy in America. Ten days later, I get a certificate of title in the mail from the courthouse. "Great, I own it," I thought. The interesting thing was I had already sold the house to a buddy of mine. We were just waiting on the certificate of title, and he was going to pay me $75,000, and I would pocket a $30,000 profit. I'm thinking I'm the smartest investor on the planet.

I received the certificate of title on Wednesday. Friday evening, I get a knock on my door and it's a process server. I didn't know that at the time. I thought it was a pizza delivery guy. He asked, "Augie Byllott?" I said, "Yes." "You've been served." The bank that held the first mortgage, which was in default, wanted the $53,000 they loaned on the property. It was very stressful.

The Lord was watching over me because it could have just as easily been a $100,000 mortgage, and I would have been in real trouble. But we were able to work with the bank that held the first mortgage. We renovated the property, sold it, and I explained to my friend who was going to buy it what happened. I said, "Look, why don't we work on the house together, and we'll split the profit whatever is left over." We ended up making about $13,000 on the deal. It taught me a very good lesson. You have to be patient and you have to do your due diligence or you're going to end up shooting yourself in the foot.

When I bought it at auction I thought I was in first position. A lot of people don't realize that the second lienholder has just as much right to foreclose as the first lienholder. The second lienholder forecloses subject to the first in its subordinate position. I really blundered by not doing thorough research. It's important that the first mortgage was relatively small. Even if they're paying off the first mortgage there was still some equity in the deal. My partner and I renovated the property and were able to sell it and eke out a meager profit.

It's not a story I'm particularly proud of other than that hopefully by sharing it with others they won't make that same mistake. I was a newbie at the time and I should have known better.

Other people can do the same thing and think they got a killer deal and find out that that first mortgage would put them underwater. What do you do? There's nothing you can do.

Tell me about being a landlord. Do you like being a landlord? Do you hate being a landlord? Why are you a landlord?

The "why" is tax benefits, cash flow, and appreciation. That's the business perspective. The fact that we buy and sell properties creates ordinary income and the benefits we get from being a landlord are depreciation and other transit allowances, which help relieve our tax burden. I like the cash flow because when you're buying and selling, your income comes in peaks and valleys even when you're doing volume. You get so much cash tied up. You want to produce a steady stream of cash flow to meet your expenses so you can stay well invested.

Amortization speaks for itself. We're killing debt and increasing equity. Appreciation is the whipped cream on the cake so to speak of it. The cherry on top.

As far as handling tenants I'm not a big fan of that, and as we've grown we've had the benefit of using property managers. We're currently using three different property managers who fit geographically. But I still have to manage the property managers.

I'm sure there are some great property managers out there who want to prove they can do the job, but finding them is a struggle and an expense, and you have to budget for it.

You need folks who are property managers, not real estate brokers that also do property management. There's a big difference between the two.

A tenant's complaint is never going to get the same level of attention as a prospective buyer's inquiry or concern. The property manager who tends to do the best job for us is one that is a dedicated property manager and does not have an active real estate agency, if you will. They focus solely on property management and do a good job.

Are you where you where you want to be?

Yes, I am where I want to be. I don't think I could have a more fulfilling life and enjoy what I do that produces income. Some people would call it work but I really enjoy what I do. If you're doing what you enjoy is it really work? I don't know. Depends on people's definition.

I enjoy the various elements and aspects of the things that I do. It involves the things I enjoy the most and as I mentioned earlier, I spent three and a half years doing the ministry. Serving others is an important element of why we're here on this planet. There was always something missing when I was doing traditional ministry because in my former career everything that I did was creative and fun.

Our real estate business has allowed me to blend the two things that I was born to do. Be creative and serve people. I have other creative talents, but wasn't born with them. I think they developed. Anyone can develop talents over time if you're willing to work at them.

I feel richly blessed to enjoy my lifestyle. To be able to serve the people that we serve, whether it's our students, whether it's our tenants, whether it's our buyers, whether it's our sellers, whomever it is that we're working with. It creates a sense of joy and peace, of fulfillment and difference. Every day is different. But not every day is peaceful, believe me.

If you're dealing with people and houses there are going to be calamities every now and then. It can get a little exciting but more often than not it's good because we're always in the state of becoming and helping others to become more than they were yesterday.

What are your goals?

We're focused on leaving a legacy. I want to continue building my portfolio and continue to help families return to homeownership. There are still a lot of people hurting from the financial crisis. With them, what we focus on is helping them get back if they want to be in a position of homeownership. We have a lot of people who rent from us. If they are good tenants for a year, I'll give them a contract for an option which gives them time to raise some additional money so that they can do a lease option and build that lease option potentially into a contract, an agreement for deed, or some kind of seller financing. If they get their credit strong enough, they can get a conventional loan and buy the property.

We're looking to help people who dream about owning their own homes. We want to make that come true. We want our tenants to have safe, clean, affordable housing. I love working with my students because we're teaching people to transform their lives by having a better understanding of money, knowing how to create it with real estate, and enjoying the fruits of their labor.

More than anything else, I'm hoping to be an example to them by paying it forward. To me that's like being a pebble in the pond. There was a time where I wanted to get to the point where I could give $100,000 a year away to charity. Now I'd much rather teach 1,000 people to make more money and have a better life. If I do that, I feel comfortable giving away $5,000 a year away to charity.

Single-family, multi-family, or commercial?

I prefer the flexibility of single-family. My bread and butter is the single-family residential. I like it because I can easily raise cash without leveraging everything.

If I have a big apartment building I usually can't sell the apartments. I like the flexibility of single-family. This could be a personal preference because I think for the right investor multi-family is a great solution.

For newbies, cutting your teeth on single-family is a lot safer, a lot easier, and a lot more achievable. It is the easiest way to build confidence and a belief system that this business really produces substantial results.

What books inspired you?

A great one that will help readers understand money is Invest In Debt by Jimmy Napier.

Another one that is excellent for people who are looking to build passive income is by David Schumacher, Buy and Hold. He's a definite get rich slowly guy. He did incredibly well.

Tell me about your PACT program.

We have two different ways that we work with investors. One is our PACT program, which stands for Personal Action Coaching and Training. That's a formal accountability based, high impact, six month coaching program. People have to go through an application and interview process in order to qualify for the program. It's six months long. It's a big commitment on everybody's part. It's a very limited audience, if you will, from the perspective that I only take ten to twelve clients at a time every six months. It's been a very successful program.

The key of it was the high impact and high accountability. It's a lot of skill development. We work on both the inner-game and the outer-game of the real estate business. We also work with you on how to build your business so that you're not just learning to work in the business but working on a business so that you have a business as opposed to just another job.

Our quick-start program is more of a go at your own pace. It's a series of home studies programs that are both CD- and DVD-based. Audio-type people can listen till their hearts are content and listen to things over and over again. For those that are more visual the DVDs work well. They cover a gamut of subjects, including lease options, buying subjects to, creating finances, exit strategies, and another component of what we call the mind-driven asking or conversations competency cash. The idea of that program is that it includes all of the scripts, questionnaires, and objections and objecting responses for our industry so people can get comfortable with what they say.

If I don't have to focus on the next thing coming out of my mouth, I can focus a lot more on what's coming out of your mouth. If I can hear what the seller's needs really are or the buyer's needs are or whatever the situation is, I'm going to be in a much better position to respond and make it a good bilateral dialogue as opposed to an interrogation, which is what a lot of investors tend to do. They fire off a series of questions and they never hear some of the more important information that might not be directly related to their question, but that can be the cue for helping them successfully work with a seller or buyer.

That program is meant to go at your own pace. It's a complete library. We also provide with that three months of e-mail support so that we don't just send you off on your own. It also comes with a four-day workshop. We hold that every October. We have two large events each year. In the fall we do our quick start intensive, which is four very intense phases of boot camp training. We also do the Rainmaker Retreat in the spring, usually April. The idea of that is we want people to learn how to become a rainmaker in their business. Rainmaker is a term originally from the legal profession, and refers to a person who brings in more business than he can personally handle. Their clients will be served by the community associates. If you want to build a large business, you're going to need people to work in your business or know what they want in business.

You can be the guy, the closer, the dealmaker, and the other people have to take care of your customers. It allows you to build the bigger business you choose. Developing skills to be a rainmaker is something that's skill-based and most people can do it if they learn to invest the time, energy and effort to make it happen.

You can learn more about Augie Byllott and the great work he does by visiting www.creatingwealthusa.com.

THOMAS MORGAN

I sat next to Thomas Morgan by chance at a Mr. Landlord conference and was impressed with his story. He is only thirty-one years old, but he has already flipped more than 300 properties as a wholesaler (and did all those deals within seven years). He is on fire and has taken control of his life and his opportunity for success. His commitment to build an empire is an example from which we can all learn.

Tell me about how you got into real estate.

I was working at a bike taxi company in Orlando, Florida, a rickshaw company, about seven years ago. I was twenty-three or twenty-four at the time. I'd get home every night at four or five in the morning and the only thing on TV was *Girls Gone Wild* and real estate infomercials. You can only watch *Girls Gone Wild* so many times. I knew the infomercials were just selling the dream, but it piqued my interest. I started looking up information on the Internet, and found a local REIA and started volunteering there because I didn't have the money to pay for their courses.

It was easy to go and there were probably three or four hundred people there at different stages of business. I just sucked it up and started going and talking to people.

How long have you been in real estate?

Seven years. My older brother and I flipped a couple small deals in Florida, just rehab stuff. I remember going to a Dave Lindahl seminar. He talks about multi-family investing and things like that. We went up to Boston and he talked about emerging markets, from this report called the Q3 report. That perked my interest because at this time Florida was crumbling in a deep recession. Everything stopped. Construction, real estate, service industry, everything. We started looking at that. We chose Chattanooga. There were a couple of different markets. Raleigh, North Carolina, Birmingham. We started digging into what was actually going on in the economies there. We discovered Chattanooga. We saw Volkswagen was building plants here, Amazon was building plants here, the Tennessee Valley Authority was growing, and a nuclear plant started putting a lot of money into retooling machines. There was a ton of money going into Chattanooga.

We started looking at the real estate market. It never really had a big spike like the rest of the country so it wasn't going to have a big decline like the rest of the country.

Our original goal was to buy apartment complexes on refinance. But the last deal we did in Florida hadn't sold, and that was most of our start-up capital. We started in wholesale to generate more leads and try to get some cash. We realized nobody was wholesaling in Chattanooga at all.

What was your defining moment?

Moving to Tennessee. At the time I didn't have a lot of cash, and I didn't really use my credit. I'd kind of been hoping on selling the house in Florida. We were supposed to make a hundred grand on it, and it just petered out. We ended up breaking even on that deal with the market crash. It was more of a "by any means necessary this has got to work."

Why did you become a wholesaler? Was that why you joined your first REIA?

At the time I wanted passive income. I was tired of working every day and not getting anywhere. I started looking at rental properties to create passive income. On paper everything looked great up here, but the houses needed a lot more work than the realtors acknowledged. I got into wholesaling because I needed quick cash. I'd always seen people talking about it, but I'd never tried it. I'd always heard you could make a lot of quick, easy money doing that.

We bought a duplex basically sight unseen, taking it subject to. It was a place where we could live in Chattanooga. It's hard to move across country if you don't have anywhere to go.

I was sitting in Orlando at a REIA meeting, bored out of my mind with some sales pitchy speaker going on. I was on craigslist, and I found the duplex. It was $10,000 down, and take over the payments. I saw an instantaneous red flag and knew it was a motivated seller. I didn't even know what a motivated seller looked like, but I knew that was a motivated seller.

I was too nervous to even call the guys. We texted back and forth. I ended up negotiating this duplex, taking over the guy's payments subject to with $5,000 down. I drove up there to look at it, and it wasn't in bad shape. It was a newer construction duplex.

We did the deal from Florida. I ended up getting one of my brother's friends to loan us the $5,000 down plus closing costs. I was told the property was cash flowing $600 a month. To me it was a no-brainer. But it wasn't getting a cash flow $600. It was only a cash flow of $450. I made a lot of rookie mistakes on that one. But was a deal. And it was no credit, and no money of mine.

How did you get the down payment down from $10,000 to $5,000?

He seemed to be motivated. I asked him what he was going to do if he kept making the payments. "What happens if you have to make the payment for another two months?"

He was in Nevada, and said, "I can't keep doing it. I can't keep making payments." After we looked at the property, I knew I could close at $5,000 down. It needed $2,000 in repairs. There was a lot more equity than we thought there was. It just worked out that way.

What advice would you give to someone just starting out?

I should have paid somebody to run real comps for me. At the time I was using Zillow and whatever free Internet resources I could get. I didn't know the market. Chattanooga's in a valley. If you look at Zillow, Zillow searches average five miles around. In Chattanooga, that covers a lot of different properties. That search pulls stuff from the bottom of the valley that's deep hood, to stuff at the top of the ridge, up on this hillside that's a million dollar house. It skews your comps very, very badly.

I shouldn't have paid as much as I did for that one. But it was cash flowing. We were taking over the note for $60,000. I want to say the payment it was $642 principle interest tax on insurance. Each side rented for $650. He was four years into a thirty-year note, so it wasn't that great of a deal taking over his note. And we still own the property.

What's the craziest thing that has happened to you as an investor?

I had a couple of crazy deals. We were buying a house from this guy. I was trying to wholesale it, and I ended up closing on it with private money and rehabbed it. About two weeks later we had a buyer lined up. We were supposed to make $28,000. The seller wanted to use a different title company than I normally use. His title company caught a notice of contract from two years ago from another investor, who had recorded a contract and clouded the title on the property. Luckily, I knew the guy who had a cloud on the title, so I called him. I said, "You never performed on this, I need you to sign off on it. I just need you to sign this release."

He said, "No, I'm not signing it. I want half the deal."

I asked, "Why do you think you deserve half my deal? You didn't fund it, you didn't rehab it, you didn't find the buyer, you didn't do anything for this. In fact, you never did anything. You didn't perform. Why would I give you half?"

I had to sue him to get him off title. He was still shooting for half the deal no matter what he did. When we were in front of the judge, I asked him why he had never closed. He didn't have an answer.

We ended up getting him thrown off the title only to end up selling it to a different buyer, but we only made $15,000 instead of the $28,000 we thought we would make.

If you had to do it over, what would you do differently?

When I first started in real estate, I owned a company, THC Investments, with my older brother and his wife. Things didn't go well. We had different business goals. He wanted to buy a lot more stuff financed, where I wanted just to start buying stuff free and clear and not have the risk and liability.

We split off our company. I took a buyout agreement with a bunch of properties. He took his properties. I started the company Momentum of Chattanooga. I've actually got to hit the reset button this year. I've got to change a lot of things in my business. It was a difficult start. It was kind of a nasty breakup between me and brother and the company. For a couple of months he took it as me attacking his wife, and I was taking it as this isn't a great business decision for either of us.

I got to change a lot of aspects. I got to reduce a lot of costs. I got to reduce a lot of my stress and headaches.

You started out partnering and now you're solo. If you could go back would you start solo?

If I had to do it all over again I'd do it solo, but I would joint-venture on the individual deals. I would never setup a company where I'm giving someone else rights. You don't know if they're going to work or not.

What are your goals?

I love wholesaling. It's a way to generate a lot of cash and provide a lifestyle. But the deal ends as soon as you pick up your check. There is no residual income. I've always liked being a landlord because it's always paid my base bills, my house, my car, everything else. At some point the market's going to shift to where I'm not going to be able to wholesale forever. I have to have a backup plan.

For 2015, my goal is if I can still wholesale $15,000 or $20,000 a month I will buy one property free and clear, once a month, or every other month. I will rehab them and rent them. Keep the cash flowing. If I can do that I will own twenty properties free and clear in two years, and I will get out. I'm looking for $15,000 passive income every month. I am 10 percent of the way there.

Tell us about your best deal.

In the past four or five months, I've raised my assignment fee standard pretty high. I used to be okay with doing 2, $3000 deals because I was doing such volume. I've kind of taken a more laid back approach lately. I just flipped a duplex. It was in Easter, Tennessee. It was a smoking deal. I went by and looked at it. It was a three-bedroom on one side, two-bedroom on the other side of a townhouse style duplex. I met with the seller and offered him $24,000 cash. Rented, it would have brought $1,400 a month. I didn't expect him to take the deal. His wife called me about two days later, and I hadn't even followed up with him. She said, "We'll take it."

I met with him end and he signed a contract. I called three buyers. One of my best friends, Cleon, looked at it and wanted it, but he didn't have cash and needed to get financed. I tagged it to my website to send to those three people, and I also tagged it Zillow. I used Freedomsoft, which tags a bunch of different websites.

A random Asian lady came to the property while I was showing it to one of my buyers. Three people in the country knew about this deal. She shows up, looks at it, and says, "I'll take it." Within ten minutes, she offered to buy it cash. I never knew this lady or anything about her. I sold it to her for $39,000. That was a quick $15,000, and I was literally in the deal maybe an hour and a half. Probably less. It closed in four days.

What do you like about the real estate business? What do you not like about it?

I love that it's a way to make a lot of money. I started doing the math, and even at $10 an hour or $20 an hour a paycheck gives me a panic attack. I could never take a vacation, and my bills would never get paid. I like the ability to work when I want. I don't always have to be out hustling. If I want to take a week off I can take a week off. As long as I have money in the bank I'm comfortable.

What I don't like about it is the fact that I'm always working, always. My girlfriend gets mad at me because my mind's always going. I'm always looking. Sometimes I feel like a crack addict. I'm always chasing the next high.

Do you have a preference between single-family, multi-family, and commercial properties?

I buy a lot of single-family residences. That's mostly all I do. I want to get into apartment complexes, because I know it's a means to an end. I want to buy twenty houses with cash over the next two years. If I buy one apartment complex I could have that many tenants, I would have to leverage the debt.

Single families offer more liquidity, but long-term wealth is going to come from multi-families and commercials.

Was there a book you liked or that motivated you to keep going?

I read *Lifeonaire* last year. It changed my goals. I used to buy a lot of stuff, anything I could keep owner-finance, subject to, or really wrapping a mortgage where I'd take it over and maybe give the seller some money. As soon as I read Lifeonaire I changed my direction. I still buy that stuff but I'm not keeping as rentals for me. I'm selling it owner-financed to somebody else. I don't have the risk or the headache of dealing with tenants. After reading Lifeonaire I decided it would be better to own twenty free and clear HUD houses at $1000 then five $100,000 houses.

What else have you been learning?

I have been studying and applying creative financing techniques. I think I own five 0 percent interest homes right now. I applied the techniques I learned and negotiated the deals the right way.

If you start buying stuff at 0 percent interest, you don't get to write off the interest on your taxes, but you will have it paid off much sooner. I bought a house up here for $9000. My payment is $150 a month for four or five years, and then I own it free and clear.

BRANDON BULL

I met Brandon while we were tutoring at Whiz Kids, a program that helps inner city kids improve their literacy. Brandon didn't have any experience investing in real estate. We became fast friends and he now has a passion for building a great portfolio. Brandon and I both want to create legacies for our families and to make an impact by donating to charities and ministries. His desire to build a better life is inspiring and will challenge you to do more deals.

How and why did you become an investor?

I grew up on a ranch in Southern Oklahoma. I came from a good family. My dad's motto was, "Give a man nine hours work for eight hours pay." He taught me the value of hard work. That's a good thought process, if you want to work for someone else your entire life. That set the tone for my education and my career.

I went to high school, did a lot of extracurricular activities, and applied for scholarships so I could go to college. I spent $40,000 on a college degree, and after I graduated I worked eighty hours a week for a construction company. I realized that I didn't want to spend all my time working for someone else. I wanted to get my time back.

I panicked and thought my fate was sealed. I quit my job, worked overseas for a while, and tried to figure out what I needed to do. I came back and found my place in Oklahoma City.

Things started to change after I started tutoring at the program you run called Whiz Kids. The program mentors kids and teaches them how to read. We met, and you introduced me to Rich Dad, Poor Dad.

That book sparked my interest in real estate investing. A lot of things will influence you and push you in different directions, including the people you surround yourself with. But that book is what changed me. I read it once, sat down and thought about it for about an hour, then picked it up and started reading it again.

What was your takeaway from Rich Dad, Poor Dad?

It reinforced the idea that I want to be wealthy, but not from the sense that I want to own a Lamborghini. I've always wanted to have enough wealth to give generously to other people, to live a comfortable lifestyle, and to own my time. To me, being wealthy means I wake up every day and go where I want to go because I can. That's the wealth that I've always wanted. I'm fighting to get that.

If you work for someone else, you work twice as hard as you're supposed to and hope that company will make you a millionaire in twenty years or whatever. Rich Dad, Poor Dad showed me there's a better way. It showed me that the house that I live in is not an asset because it costs me money. It completely changed the way I looked at the things I bought.

I began to surround myself with investors who could influence me, slowly de-risk the real estate business, and help me get in the game.

What motivated you to buy your first property?

It took me about five months after I read the book until I really decided I was going to change things. My company told me I couldn't do Whiz Kids anymore. They said that because it was during "work hours" I would have to stop volunteering. Keep in mind, I worked well over fifty hours a week and travelled extensively. I had been given permission to participate.

They said, "Sorry. Even though we said you could do this, you can't do it anymore." It dawned on me that as long as I worked for someone else I would have to do what they told me to do. That was the tipping point. That's when I said, "I'm going to change."

I started researching. I started talking to people who understood the business. I started asking them about investing in real estate and tried to understand. I knew it would have been a bad decision to just take my cash and go buy a house. I knew that was wrong.

I didn't know how to buy, and I didn't know where to buy. I didn't know what to rent, and I didn't how to manage it. I began to surround myself with people who knew the business. I began to read books that people recommended and just started working my way through things I didn't understand.

Can you tell us about your first deal?

One of my friends from Southern Oklahoma knows how to spot a deal. He has always been an entrepreneur, and I had to change my mindset so that I could understand the deals he was talking about. We are from the same town and felt comfortable buying properties in certain neighborhoods. We grew up there and we know the area. One of the things that slowed me down when I moved to Oklahoma City was buying in the wrong places, but that's a story for another day.

My friend and I talked about it for thirty days, and we blasted out numbers and tried to buy houses. We put in several offers. We were within a few thousand dollars on a couple. We won some, only to be told we didn't really win. Then they kicked us out of the auctions.

I learned many online auction companies aren't trying to sell properties. All they're doing is finding out how much their properties are worth to investors. We won one auction and planned to flip the property for $40,000. But when we tried to close, they told us, "We decided not to sell." They could never bring the title up. It was a waste of time, and I had to get nasty with them. I got my earnest money back, but at the end of the day, it cost me 500 bucks for an appraisal. To me, that's a very inexpensive learning experience in real estate.

It took another two or three months until I'd stumbled into the first property I was able to buy. By the time all that shook out, I learned it was a mistake to purchase real estate investments with a partner who was as much of a rookie as I was. We needed more experience at the table.

Partners can be a bad decision. You've got to make sure that you both bring good things to the table and have a good contract.

Eventually, a wholesaler I met found a deal and sent it to me. But being the pokey newbie I was, I sat on it. I looked at it and sat on it for about three days. Within those three days, someone else had it under contract.

It turns out that other investor was you. You were kind enough to back out, and I bought my first property.

What are your goals?

I have learned how important it is to set goals. I never set goals until 2015. I have goals for this year. I want to buy ten properties, and not just any ten properties. I want to have ten properties that average a 30 percent return on investment and that cash flow at least 200 bucks a month each. And I want to do it with my cash.

I thought about saying I want $200 a month cash flow per unit, but what would it cost me to get there? I built myself some constraints, saying, "I can get $200 a month cash flow, but it has to be a 30 percent return on the cash I have in it." If I have a no-money-down deal, I don't care if it's $100 a month because I will cash flow forever. But if I borrow money I want $200 a month or a 30 percent return. Even better, I want both.

I've already refinanced the first property I bought. I bought it for $26,000. It appraised for $38,000. I only financed $20,000 of it. Then I have $6,000 in repairs. I've got about $10,000. All in, I'm in this project for about $32,000. My payment with taxes, insurance, and fees is $250 a month. I also pay someone to manage it. It rents for $625 a month so the return's good, and the cash flow is there. My annual return is about 32 percent.

You entered the real estate investing with the idea of being completely hands-off. What's your philosophy on that?

I have a full-time job. After working around you and being around other investors, I realized you can manage your own properties. There's a guy in my neighborhood who has five houses. He's worked the same job for thirty-five years, and he manages them by himself. But I want my business to grow. I want to buy my time back. When I started investing, I wore myself out trying to figure out how to manage property before I decided my time is better spent getting my W-2 and working for a company. I focus my time and energy on finding deals.

In the future, I want to spend all my time with my family, mentor, and give back to the community. For now, I will pay someone to manage my properties until I can get in the game 100 percent and then consider managing them myself, if I want to.

What advice would you give to someone starting out?

When things are looking bleak, remember there's always going to be another deal. Calm down, don't panic, and don't buy a house just to say you have a house or a property. There will always be another deal. Spend some time, whether it's thirty days or six months, understanding the business. Surround yourself with people who know the business, read some key books, and get ready to advance. But don't spend too much time before you buy or you will become complacent. Remember to have some coaching and guidance before you sign a check.

Your background is in construction management. You know how to manage crews. Has that helped you in real estate?

No. It's hurt me. I'm too process-focused to my expectations. The way you work with a commercial contractor is totally different from how you deal with a residential or landlord type of contractor. The means in which you meet and discuss the scope, the means in which you pay them, how they get materials, and what their expectations are all involve negotiation. There's no paperwork, there's no formal follow up, no punch list, and no checklist, which is not what I am used to.

I walk through projects and make a list. I talk about my list of what needs to be done with the contractor, and I don't pay him until the work is done.

It has been a learning process. It's a switch from commercial construction to residential repair. It's not that one is better than the other. They are just different. It's a different group of people, and you speak to them differently.

How many deals have you reviewed?

I've looked at and analyzed well over 100 units. Sometimes I look at one property several times, and I get confused and frustrated. I say, "I will never buy this," and then I talk to someone who looks at it from a different angle. Within a minute my perspective has changed and I think, "I can buy that."

How do you find new properties?

I do a few different things. I try to drive around and find "For sale by owner" signs. That's a different approach for me. I'm trying to get better at cold calling FSBO sellers.

The main way I find properties is through a couple of realtors who send me listings that are within my parameters. I look for houses that are listed for less than $75,000, and I look at the neighborhoods they're in. I'm learning more about the neighborhoods in Oklahoma City, and that helps me. I am a cash flow buyer and my priorities are cash flow, asset integrity, and location.

Once I look at a house, I find out who owns it and understand if they're an investor or if they're an actual individual owner, because you speak to those two types of owners differently. I try to learn if they're motivated or not by the mortgages on the property or if they've already moved out-of-state. If the owner lives at a different address, and there are there two mortgages, there are two payments. That can make a lot of difference when it comes time to haggle about price.

Then I'll e-mail the realtor and begin to structure my offer. I won't put a number in there, but let them know who I am and that I am an investor. I don't say that I buy in that area, but I say I'm very interested and I follow the area. I ask if the seller is firm on his price or if he would consider a more reasonable offer from an investor's perspective.

That's my foot-in-the-door. If they reply back and say, "No, this is a good home. We'll get retail," then I move on. I don't waste my time. If they say, "Yes, the seller will entertain any offers," I keep going.

I say, "I'm an investor, a cash flow buyer. Here's what it would take for it to cash flow for me." I'll break down the details including my cash flow and expenses. I'll send it that way. If I never hear back from them, so be it, but sometimes I do.

How long have you been investing in real estate?

I bought my first house in October 2014. So four months.

What mistakes have you made?

After I bought my first property, I immediately started looking for the next one. But I didn't have any tenants in the first house. I jacked around with my rehab. It wasn't even a rehab. It was some paint touch-ups, some minor repairs, and a little bit of flooring. I spent so much time trying to find people to do it cheap. The property needed some paint touch-up, a hot water tank replacement, a little bit of flooring, a good cleaning, and a few miscellaneous plumbing repairs. It took me three months, which is terrible. Once you catch a fish you've got to get it in the boat, and I had a hard time reeling in the first one. As soon as you hook a fish, you've got to reel it in before you cast your line and catch another one.

Single, multi, or commercial? What are your thoughts?

I would love to be in commercial someday, only because I'm exposed to a lot of commercial leases in my job. Those investors make serious money, but that's a whole other game. Single-family is what I'm tackling for now. I'm going to focus on that. I'll do duplexes. I might even do a fourplex, but it'd have to be a smoking deal for me to buy a fourplex.

Here is a ranching reference for you. Is it better to slaughter the calf or milk the cow?

As long as the cow is producing milk, you'd milk the cow. It's like a rental property. As long as that house has a tenant who pays the rent, do it. As long as it's producing, keep repairing and renting it. Houses are cows. Milk them until they go dry. It's hard to go broke when you're making money.

GLOSSARY OF QUESTIONS

About the Authors

Steven R. VanCauwenbergh is a long-time investor in income-producing properties and has mastered the critical areas of purchasing, financing, renovating and managing real estate. He has authored several books and courses empowering people to reach their goals of financial freedom. He is a highly sought after personal coach and teaches his techniques in seminars across the country.

Walter B. Jenkins is the proud father of international hockey sensation Katie Jenkins. Before beginning his career as a writer and speaker, Walter was an attorney and sports agent. He now helps people turn their ideas into great books. In his spare time he enjoys studying tae kwon do, scuba diving, riding his bike, and training his German shepherd, Jake the wonder dog. Learn more at www.walterbjenkins.com.

the savvy

LANDLORD

CONNECT AT:

thesavvylandlordbook.com

Freebies

Down-loadable Forms

New Products

Tips

Blog

Twitter: twitter.com/landlordbook
Facebook: facebook.com/thesavvylandlord
Email: info@thesavvylandlordbook.com

★ Whiz Kids
O K L A H O M A
—— A Division of City Care ——

The mission of Whiz Kids is to improve the well-being of inner-city youth through academic tutoring and positive mentoring relationships.

About Whiz Kids

Founded in 1996, under the umbrella of the 501(c) 3 nonprofit, City Care, Inc., Whiz Kids is a nonprofit, one-on-one, tutoring and mentoring program for at-risk students in the Oklahoma City metropolitan area. Whiz Kids collaboratively and creatively addresses Oklahoma City's urban social and educational crisis by matching tutor/mentors with at-risk students. Teachers select students for the Whiz Kids program because they are reading below their grade level and can benefit from a mentoring relationship. Tutors are paired with a child and meet weekly with the same child during the school year for a one-on-one after-school tutoring session. Whiz Kids sites are churches in each school's community that donate their facility and provide tutors and on-site coordinators. These urban churches are partnered with other metro area (typically suburban) churches to provide additional volunteers and tutors, essentially bringing the resource of people back to the urban neighborhoods where the children live. Each site has a liaison teacher from the school that serves as an educational consultant, and is a resource for the volunteer tutors.

In order to qualify for the Whiz Kids program, a school must have at least 87% of its students eligible for free/reduced lunch. Seventeen of the Whiz Kids schools have percentages higher than 95% free/reduced lunch and four are 100% free/reduced lunch. Because of this, Whiz Kids serves children who live in some of Oklahoma City's most desperate neighborhoods, where poverty, illiteracy and violence often strangle a child's promise. The schools served by the Whiz Kids program are mostly Oklahoma City Public Schools, but also include a few schools in the Crooked Oak, Putnam City, Mid-Del and Crutcho districts.

Since its inception, one school and a handful of volunteers, Whiz Kids has grown to serve more than 800 students from 29 at-risk elementary schools, in partnership with 63 churches.

Get involved and make an impact!

www.whizkidsok.org

www.savvyinvestors.com

www.ingramcontent.com/pod-product-compliance
Lightning Source LLC
Chambersburg PA
CBHW071700200326
41519CB00012BA/2575